Contents

About the author

Dr Neil Harris is an experienced careers adviser and author. Previously Director of the University College London Careers Service, he specialises in advising scientists and engineers on their career development and employers on their recruitment of technologists.

Starting his career in research and development in the metals and turbine industries, Neil became a research fellow at Liverpool University before moving on to career counselling. He wrote the *New Scientist* careers column for 12 years and many books including *Getting into Engineering* and *Getting into IT and the Internet*. In 2000 he set up Lifelines Personal Development Ltd, which provides career guidance and has given many skills workshops to undergraduate and PhD scientists and engineers at the Institute of Biology, the Institution of Mechanical Engineers, Imperial College and elsewhere.

Acknowledgements

Thanks are due to the following for their assistance in updating the information contained in this fourth edition of *Careers with a Science Degree*: The Royal Society for many helpful hints; UCAS for assistance with statistics; Joint Council for Qualifications for advice on statistics; Professor Michael Elves, previously of GS K and adviser to the House of Commons Science and Technology Committee; Professor Svein Sjøberg of the University of Oslo (of the Science and Scientists Project); pupils of Aloeric School, Melksham.

What do Graduates Do? 2005 published by AGCAS/ Graduate Prospects. The data in *What do Graduates do?* is derived from the Higher Educational Statistics Agency (HESA) *Destinations of Leavers from Higher Education* survey.

Thanks also to Jane Antrobus, Richard Cary, Mike Gilbert, David Long, Andy Malone, Rachel McCoy, Mike Partridge, Paul Pilkington, Diana Robertson, Sarah Polack, Bob Simpson and Sally Sunderland for their cooperation and providing the careers profiles on such a broad range of careers. Special gratitude to all those who contributed to earlier editions of this book including Mary Munro, Eileen De'Ath, Tessa Doe and Debbie Steel, many of whose words still make a valuable contribution.

4538900

U

D

areers with a Science Degree

Neil Harris

This bc
self so

Student Helpbook Series

Lifetime Careers

Careers with a Science Degree – fourth edition

Published by Lifetime Careers Publishing, 7 Ascot Court, White Horse Business Park, Trowbridge BA14 0XA

© Lifetime Careers Wiltshire Ltd, 2006

ISBN 1 904979 07 6 ✓

ISBN-13 978 190497907 4

Printed and bound by Cromwell Press Ltd, Trowbridge
Cover design by Lesley May
Illustrations by Joe Wright

Chapter one
Why science?

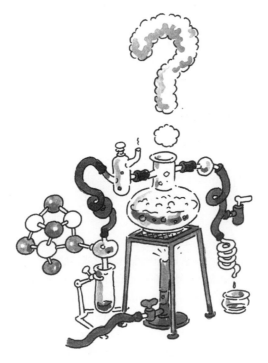

This chapter covers:

- the value of science to individuals and society

- the usefulness of science education in career terms

- current and future issues facing scientists

- some of the myths about science that need dispelling!

'Our ambition is for Britain to become the science capital of the world, to become a world leader in exploiting knowledge, to become the most supportive environment in the world. A place where scientists everywhere want to come and work. We are well on the way. We should have the confidence to recognise that science can be a force for good and to grasp the opportunities that it presents to us. The UK can be a leader in stem cell research, biotechnology, etc. The UK can continue to create a climate where this sort of research can flourish. We need to foster innovation and enterprise. We must equip people with the skills they need to prosper in a dynamic modern economy.'

Tony Blair, 17 November 2004

A valuable tool

Science is fascinating. It engages our curiosity about why our world is as it is and how things work. Solving scientific problems develops our ingenuity. No matter how much we discover about our world there is always much more to be discovered. Scientific investigation never ends.

Scientific understanding is of great value – to individuals and to society as a whole – in many areas of modern life. Whether our interest lies in researching groundbreaking scientific ideas or developing new products, whether it takes the form of concern for our impact on the environment, crucial issues of health and safety and world health problems, or is simply a natural curiosity about what things are made of and how they work, science is important to us all.

Taking a science degree does not mean that you are choosing to spend the rest of your life working in a laboratory. Many science graduates want to be lab-based, hands-on scientists but there are lots of others who use their science degree as a stepping stone into other careers. Science graduates can go into most things that other graduates do, and many more. They can consider job areas where a science degree is essential and those where scientific knowledge is an advantage, as well as the 50% plus of graduate vacancies which are open to graduates of any discipline.

Most of us will change our career direction several times in our working lives. A science degree gives you the most options to choose from. Einstein was a teacher, a patent agent and a researcher during his career. Most scientists change their roles as their careers progress. Many career and postgraduate study opportunities are open to holders of Higher National Diplomas as well as to honours degree graduates. Some students are now graduating with two-year foundation degrees which were partly designed by employers, so should be well accepted by them – and, if completed successfully, like HNDs they can be converted to an honours degree by further study (See Chapter five, page 109).

What this book is about

This book will help you to connect science subjects to the wide range of job choices open to science, maths and technology graduates. It encourages you to reflect upon some of the stereotypical images of science and scientists in Britain, to look beyond them to the real challenges and great opportunities that science offers. It takes a look at science globally, and helps you to understand the fast-changing world of graduate employment.

The subject choices you make at school have an immediate effect on the range of jobs that are open to you. If dropped after GCSE, science subjects can be difficult to take up again at a later stage. Too often, when people come to apply for higher education they find their choices are limited by decisions they made when they were younger. That is why this book is important to you now, whether you are in year 9 or about to start your higher education. Different parts of the book are relevant to different stages of your education.

Science is different

Why does this book focus on the sciences rather than all the other subjects people study at school and college? Why is science different?

■ Science is about concepts and ideas. Your knowledge and understanding of science builds up gradually. Understanding new concepts often means building on what you have already learned and understood. This is why you cannot usually go on to science

A level or BTEC National courses without studying sciences at GCSE. Similarly, in Scotland you would not normally expect to take a science for Highers or Advanced Highers unless you had already done well in the subject.

■ Scientific concepts are much easier to learn when you are younger. This is particularly true in mathematics, the essential tool of all science. But it also applies to physics, chemistry and biology.

Science isn't a dead end

There are those in research and academic jobs who will continue to work at the frontiers of science throughout their working lives. You may enjoy investigating in the laboratory and have insatiable curiosity about why things are as they are, but with a science degree you are never trapped in a particular career. Many people with science degrees find that they become gradually less concerned with new scientific concepts as their careers progress. Some go on to take further qualifications in other areas, such as financial or human resource management, marketing and sales or technical writing. Often in these jobs they still use the analytical and problem-solving skills they developed when studying science.

It is much easier to move from jobs that require a high level of scientific knowledge into those that require you to develop knowledge, skills and experience, than it is to move in the opposite direction. So, if you are going to study science either for a long-term career or as a basis on which to build other skills, now is the time to do it! Take some time to think about it seriously.

Don't miss the boat!

Once you have stopped studying science it is very difficult to go back to it. If you don't take science at A level or equivalent it can be harder to get into science in higher education. For those who want to get into science having not studied science A levels, some universities and colleges run **foundation** courses which lead to a place on a science degree course at that institution. They are for students aged 19+ whose

A level subjects are a poor match for the degree course they want; they are also aimed at those who are returning to education after a break and students from overseas who need to improve their English language skills before embarking on a science degree course.

There are also **Access** courses. These are run by further education colleges and are specifically designed for students who were, for whatever reason, unable to do well in science at school and want to return to study. Access courses can be taken over one year, full-time or two years, part-time. Access to science courses are aimed at those wanting to study science at higher education level, and success can lead to entry onto a science degree course.

If you don't study a higher education course in science you are very unlikely to be able to follow a career in science at a professional level, or take a science-related postgraduate course. This is quite different from other areas like business, accountancy, social work or even law, where many people with degrees in other subjects (including the sciences) go on to make successful careers.

■ Find out about the wide range of careers open to science graduates.

■ Avoid shutting off any career routes which you may later want to reconsider.

■ Try to allow enough flexibility to enable you to develop new interests and skills.

The decision to drop science can be very hard to reverse later on. It's almost a one-way intellectual escalator!

Looking beyond Frankenstein

Although the study of science is a very positive development in which people continually seek novel ideas and aim to move forward the frontiers of knowledge, there are those who project negative images and stereotypes. A stereotype is an image that is fixed and is not changed by discussion or persuasion. You may find a grain of truth in some stereotypes, but it is usually buried under layers of ignorance and prejudice.

People have preconceived ideas of science being difficult, boring, inhuman, laboratory-based and – despite decades of equal opportunities – a career for men. The image that lingers of Dr Frankenstein as an isolated male manufacturer of monsters is very powerful. Debates about genetically modified crops, stem-cell research and 'scientists playing God' still evoke this stereotype.

Dr Frankenstein, a fictional character created in 1818 by Mary Shelley, is an idealistic young scientist who finds the secret of giving life to matter. He creates a living being from parts of dead bodies, but the creature looks so hideous that he is feared and persecuted by those who meet him. The monster therefore becomes embittered and cruel and turns against his creator. It is extraordinary that this fictitious person has remained such a powerful influence for so long.

Chapter two of this book is about the image of science and scientists, where these perceptions come from and how they affect subject choice.

Science as a subject

There is a very close association in many people's minds between science the subject and science the career. In some countries people think of their career as a natural progression through qualifications and into a related occupation. In the UK, USA and many countries of the British Commonwealth, however, we are much more flexible in the way we can change the direction of our careers. Those choosing to study history are seldom influenced by their image of a historian! Few students of French imagine themselves as French professors or interpreters. People usually choose arts and humanities subjects because they are interested in them or because they are good at them, not necessarily because they lead to a particular career. Why should science be any different? There are many other areas besides a career in scientific research where you can use scientific knowledge and skills.

We should think of science as an important part of our general education, as it is considered in many other countries. The fact that it is a compulsory part of the National Curriculum until year 11 gives everyone the chance to gain some understanding of what science is about.

Is science difficult?

When people miss out on a few classes for some reason, or just come up against something they find difficult to understand, they often become discouraged and lose interest. This is particularly true of science subjects because of the way you build up knowledge and understanding. If you do start to fall behind in science or maths, it is vital to ask for help and support straight away, because it can be difficult to recover if you leave the problem unresolved for too long.

You may find the concepts and ideas in one science subject harder than in another. Everyone is different in the way they approach subjects. There are people who find maths and physics so easy that they can't see why other people find it a struggle, but they are the exception! Most people find difficulties with some concepts at some stage, and need to make an extra effort to get back in the swim.

Some people find mathematics and physics harder than chemistry. Others find chemistry much more difficult than biology. People who enjoy biology and do very well at it may not be confident in mathematics. Others prefer a topic-based approach, such as environmental science, where they find they can understand the concepts more easily because they are applied to a specific area or problem.

Science concepts are not just 'common sense'. Most people find that they have to work to understand the basic concepts of science before they feel confident enough to join in a discussion on scientific ideas. Try not to let the difficulty of the basic concepts put you off science because, once you have conquered these, you can reach the much more rewarding and highly creative aspects of the subject.

Is science boring?

It shouldn't be. Science is like learning to play a musical instrument: the longer you work at it the more satisfaction it will give you and the more creative you can be. If science at school is taught well, it should convey the excitement of having ideas and testing them out, the joy of exercising your curiosity to discover why or how things happen as they do.

Science at GCSE level is changing. Pilot schemes, called 21ˢᵗ Century Science, which began in 2003, have been successful. These, together with the Government White Paper on 14-19 Education, will shake up the teaching of science, making it much more interesting and relevant to today's technological society.

The science curriculum is being improved to make it more relevant and up-to-date. It will be much more difficult to be bored. There will be courses that cover the core subjects designed to 'give everyone the scientific literacy they need as citizens in a society where science and technology play a key part in shaping our lives'. However, if you want to aim for a career that uses your science, you will have the opportunity to take additional science at GCSE. If you are much more interested in applying science than being immersed in lots of theory, there is also the option to take applied science as a double GCSE subject. That route offers the opportunity to see how science is applied in industry, pharmaceuticals, energy, medicine, telecommunications, etc.

Because science is a fast-changing field, and every new discovery leads to new theories and new concepts, the science being taught on school and university courses is continually developing. You will learn about developments in genetics and astronomy that people who were at school or college when your parents were young had never heard of! It seems incredible, for example, that in 2005 a previously unknown planet of our solar system has been discovered.

Alongside scientific changes, there have been huge developments in information and communications technology. Computers have enabled scientists to develop highly sophisticated instruments, to store and analyse huge quantities of data and to make scientific models and simulations. They can use scientific databases on the other side of the world and communicate with each other through email and the internet. The huge development of computer graphics helps scientists to communicate ideas, not only within the scientific community but also outside it.

Is science narrow?

When you leave your degree course you will know more about your subject, and have greater skills in computing and information technology, than people who left a similar course ten years ago. You will have marketable up-to-date knowledge and technical ability, as well as all the other qualities that employers expect of graduates, such as analytical, team-working, communication, research and problem-solving skills.

The employment situation is very different for someone with a degree in English literature or history. There are very few jobs where the content of these courses is immediately useful. Arts graduates have to rely on other more general skills or take vocational training courses when developing their careers. Science graduates can do almost all the jobs that arts graduates go into – particularly if they have good communication skills – with the added advantage of being able to use their scientific knowledge, either directly or indirectly.

Science is international

Another thing that is different about science is its internationalism. Scientific ideas and applications are not limited by national boundaries, or by local custom and practice. You will see in some of the career profiles featured in this book (e.g. Sarah Polack page 168, Rachel McCoy page 149, Bob Simpson page 117 and Jane Antrobus page 134) that science graduates can find job opportunities overseas, as well as opportunities to study and collaborate with scientists from other countries. Some universities offer science degrees that include experience of working or studying abroad. There are also chances to study abroad through exchange schemes at school, and by choosing a higher education course which includes a period overseas, such as with the EU's Socrates-Erasmus scheme. UK students are entitled to study at EU universities for their entire course, if their language skills are up to it! And opportunities are by no means restricted to Europe: Jane Antrobus's and Sarah Polack's profiles (pages 133 and 168) show that!

Organisations such as the International Association for the Exchange of Students for Technical Experience (IAESTE) help science students to get vacation work abroad during their degree studies.

Through the internet and email, scientists are aware of the work of others and are in constant contact with colleagues around the world. This global outlook is a feature of the science departments at most universities and will be a useful asset even if you go into non-scientific work after your higher education.

The international nature of science means that there are many opportunities for science graduates to work or study overseas at some stage of their careers. International organisations, world trade and commerce also create opportunities to travel and work abroad. One of the aims of the European Commission is to enhance the mobility of scientists between EU member states.

Science opens doors

Taking a science degree is clearly not just a route into being a highly qualified lab assistant. There are many ways to become involved in science without doing practical laboratory work. On the other hand, many scientists complain that they don't get enough time in their laboratories!

A science degree is a starting point for a lot of different career routes. It is a general education which will help you to understand some of the most crucial issues affecting the future of this planet.

There has been a huge increase in popular interest in and debate about scientific developments, particularly in medical and biological research and in computer applications.

There is an increasing demand and need for good communicators who understand scientific developments and their likely impact. This need, together with the information technology explosion, has opened up exciting new career developments in and around science. Science is definitely not for the inarticulate.

Most of the information about careers for science graduates divides the opportunities into three groups:

1. careers using specialist scientific knowledge

2. careers using general scientific knowledge and other qualities or skills

3. careers using mostly the other benefits of your science education (ICT, numeracy, logic, problem solving, etc).

Most science graduates have jobs from these different groups at different stages of their careers. But again the 'one-way escalator' effect means that most people move in the direction of 1 to 3, and many start at 2 or 3.

Richard Cary

Richard Cary demonstrates how, by taking different options, you can use the flexibility of some science degree courses to gain knowledge in the area where you want your career to go. (See also Andy Malone page 182.) He started as a laboratory scientist but developed into a role that involves international negotiations in Europe.

Career profile

Job title: regulatory scientist

Employer: The Health and Safety Executive

A levels: maths, chemistry, physics, biology

Degree: BSc in biochemistry

University: Royal Holloway College, University of London

'I became very keen on science when I first started studying it at school. I enjoyed biology most. I got the impression from my teacher that I was no good at physics and my results would be poor, so I worked hard and got an A!

My mother had worked in the medical profession as a nurse and talking to her got me interested in becoming a biochemist. When I was sixteen I decided that would be the career for me. I had a clear sense that science was interesting, the place to be and a good career to follow. Totally convinced that I wanted to be a scientist, I easily decided to take biology, maths, physics and chemistry at A level. Practical work in the laboratory was always something I enjoyed and the more of it the better as far as I was concerned. My leaning was towards biology and chemistry rather than physics and maths.

When the time came to apply for a place at university there was only one subject that I was interested in studying. That was biochemistry and I also chose to study at Royal Holloway College, part of the University of London but way out in Egham, near Windsor. It was a modular degree, so I was able to pick and choose many of the subjects I studied. Organic, inorganic and physical chemistry were compulsory but I was able to take courses in botany and cell biology. At that time I was extremely interested in the biochemistry of plants and my final year project was on isolating and purifying a plant enzyme. Then I had to assay it to check what I ended up with. I was in the lab every afternoon, following two hours of lectures most mornings and I enjoyed almost all of it.

During my final year I made lots of job applications but opportunities for plant biologists were non-existent. I eventually joined a Medical Research Council laboratory in Carshalton as a trainee toxicologist, where I investigated cancer of the oesophagus. Later I joined Huntingdon Research, a laboratory that does contract research for industry, and that broadened my experience as a general toxicologist. The work involved investigating agrochemicals, pesticides and pharmaceuticals and managing toxicology studies to check the risk of their causing cancer.

Now I'm employed as a regulatory scientist at the Health and Safety Executive in Bootle. When I began work there I was assessing study reports on various compounds and summarising the toxicology studies. We were looking for the effects of substances on reproduction and also how people could be sensitised to individual substances that they were exposed to at work. I would spend six months or more investigating one substance, deciding what the hazards were and how it should be classified and labelled.

Now we have a different strategy. We look at diseases and the substances that cause them rather than start with the substances. My job is to discover occupational carcinogens and try to rank their danger levels.

My career has given me a high level of responsibility. The Health and Safety Executive is a thoroughly good place to work and I have had the opportunity to represent it internationally and in Europe. I like being academically challenged, which happens constantly. There is a tremendous sense of learning so much all of the time.'

Only you can choose

Information about careers and jobs comes to you from many different sources and you have been absorbing it ever since you were very young. Now you are able to be more discriminating and can look more critically at the information you pick up, whether formally or informally. You are able to question and assess information and opinion, to judge how relevant it is now or how useful it will be to your situation in the future. Certainly, if you are going to be a scientist you will need to assess data critically. Ask yourself how the information was collected, by whom and to what end.

Things change. Is the current interest in and importance of your subject likely to be the same in four or five years' time when you finish your degree course? New opportunities may arise which do not yet exist. Bioinformatics, nanotechnology and biometrics are three subjects that have only recently become important. New influences, both economic and social, could affect the prospects for scientists by the time you are in your twenties or thirties.

You will change too. You will develop new skills and interests. You may find you are much better than you thought at some things which you now find difficult. You could find you are brilliant at something you have not even tried yet!

Your values will change. You might find, for example, that you become passionately involved in some environmental issue and need some knowledge of chemistry to understand the problem or contribute to a solution. You might be attracted to a particular career now because you have heard the starting salaries are good. But what happens after the first few years? Will you continue to be interested in the job? Will it seem worthwhile? Will you be able to progress and will your skills be useful in other areas later on?

There are no easy answers to any of these questions. But it's no use doing nothing and sticking your head in the sand, hoping it will all turn out right in the end. It's your career, and you are the best person to have control of it. Take time to look at all the options.

This book will help you to ask the right questions of yourself and other people. It is a starting point for your decisions about science subjects at A level and equivalent, and in higher education.

Science in the future

The past few years have seen cloning, the mapping of the human genome, landings on Mars, energy from wind and wave power and other remarkable advances. Predictions of scientific breakthroughs in the near future include:

- greater understanding of the nature of dark matter

- nanoscience/nanotechnology – the development of products the size of a nanometre (a millionth of a millimetre) – will result in even further miniaturisation of electrical circuits

- advances in the use of computer models to predict climate change more accurately

- stem cell research and the growing of human tissue

- further investigation into fusion energy and other sources of clean, safe alternatives to carbon-based fuels.

However, Sir Harry Kroto, Nobel prizewinner in 1996, has pointed out that important discoveries in science are usually totally unpredictable. That's what makes them important!

Science graduates tell their stories

Throughout this book you will find profiles of science graduates at different stages of their careers, explaining the subject choices they made and their career paths so far. The profiles are genuine stories of people with degrees or diplomas in scientific, technological and mathematical subjects. As you read through the book you will find that some of the things they say have also been quoted in the relevant sections. The profilees are:

Richard Cary – page 15

(biochemistry graduate, now a regulatory scientist)

Richard decided from an early age that he wanted to be a scientist, possibly concerned with medical issues. He used his flexible biochemistry degree to improve his knowledge of chemistry and also to begin his understanding of toxicology. After a stint checking whether agrochemicals and pesticides are safe, correctly labelled and categorized, he moved to the Health and Safety Executive, where he investigates the health implications of working with various substances.

Sally Sunderland – page 60

(civil engineering graduate, now site agent for a huge bridge building scheme at Paddington Station)

Sally thought civil engineering sounded exciting, and didn't want to be office-bound. She says, 'From the experience I've gained, I would advise anyone to study science and maths in preparation for an engineering degree course. In engineering you meet such a wide range of people and have a varied career. You certainly can't get bored!'

David Long – page 97

(astrophysics graduate, now a reactor control engineer in a nuclear power station)

David was 'intrigued by the seemingly mind-expanding theories and obvious applications of physics'. He loved 'the practical side and enjoyed long afternoons playing in the laboratory' while at university.

Bob Simpson – page 117

(marine biology graduate with a passion for diving)

Bob says, 'I chose my degree course because it offered the opportunity for diving during the third year. I joined the university diving club and qualified in diving. I've worked in aqua centres both in Scotland and the USA. In my spare time I breed animals and fish. Lately I have got into breeding pythons.'

Paul Pilkington – page 120

(physics graduate, now a lead engineer with Airbus)

Paul studied physics although he always intended to go into engineering, because: 'At school ... I was always taking things apart and putting them back together again.' Now he's testing the A380 Airbus in Toulouse.

Diana Robertson – page 130

(maths graduate who opted for a career as a maths teacher)

'Science was my best subject at school,' says Diana. 'I found maths interesting and challenging. I decided to qualify as a teacher. Some of the children were unruly and I nearly quit. But I found that, as a maths teacher, I was in demand and there were plenty of good schools to choose between.'

Jane Antrobus – page 133

(environmental science and geography graduate, now an environmental planner)

Jane says her job may 'not be commonly perceived as "scientific", but this demonstrates that a science-based education can provide access to a wide range of career paths.'

Mike Partridge – page 147

(natural sciences graduate, now a research physicist for the Institute of Cancer Research and the Royal Marsden NHS Trust)

Mike chose a wide-ranging degree course because he was unsure about his career ambitions when he left school, but can now happily say, 'I find academic work in medical physics uniquely stimulating and rewarding. The mixture of clinical work, student supervision, teaching and research makes the job varied and demanding. My work involves regular travel, lecturing on courses and at conferences around the world ...'

Rachel McCoy– page 149

(chemistry graduate with a PhD, now a senior research scientist in pharmaceuticals)

Rachel enjoyed biology at A level but took a degree in chemistry. Later she did a PhD and got into research both in the UK and USA. She combined her interest in biology and chemistry by studying chemical pharmacology and now works on studies of urinary diseases for Pfizer. She says, 'the equipment here is first class. I'm like a kid with a new toy.'

Sarah Polack – page 168

(biological sciences graduate, now a research assistant with the London School of Hygiene and Tropical Medicine studying for her PhD)

Sarah narrowed down a general interest in biology to a special interest in public health during her studies. This has led her into research projects in Africa. 'I will be working in Tanzania for some of the year, evaluating the impact of a water supply on the disease trachoma. In addition, I shall be involved in a project mapping the global distribution of trachoma using GIS [geographic information systems]. I think a science-based education is extremely valuable as it can lead you into so many different directions.'

Andy Malone – page 182

(geology graduate, now working as a development geoscientist for BP)

'I decided to go for a physics degree', says Andy, 'but physical geography was my most enjoyable subject at school. Eventually, I left the physics behind and concentrated on geology. The field trips were hugely enjoyable and I gained a good knowledge of tectonics and palaeontology. Now I'm analysing geophysical and geological data to assess the economic viability of oil fields.'

Mike Gilbert – page 185

(natural sciences graduate, now a partner in a firm of solicitors specialising in intellectual property)

Having been introduced to the idea of intellectual property by his university careers adviser, Mike qualified as a solicitor and 'rapidly became heavily involved in highly scientific cases concerning pharmaceutical patent disputes, chemical patent matters, industrial espionage and breach of confidence cases. All of these cases have involved me using the scientific knowledge I have built up over the years.'

Footnote: The afore-mentioned Nobel Prize winner, Sir Harry Kroto, is also quoted as saying that the decline in engineering students in the UK is connected to the demise of the Meccano set. Discuss!

Chapter two
The image of science and scientists

This chapter covers:

- images of science and scientists in Britain
- primary and secondary school pupils' views on science
- advanced level subject and degree subject choices
- changes ahead.

Just imagine

When you picture a scientist, do you think of someone who is:

male	female
old	young
brainy	stupid
hardworking	lazy
scruffy	smart
precise	muddled
ingenious	unimaginative
practical	ethereal
kind	mean
dull	fun
rich	poor
cold	friendly
outgoing	shy
a back-room person	a leader
creative	plodding
tone-deaf	musical

We are all influenced by stereotypes, and not just when it comes to scientists. Science seems such an unknown quantity to many people that, as a result, some very strong stereotypes have emerged to depict the people who study and work in the area. The two most common caricatures are the eccentric boffin – brought to life on TV by personalities like David Bellamy, Adam Hart-Davis, Heinz Woolf and Patrick Moore – and the evil professor intent on destroying his enemies and ruling the world – fortunately found only in fiction!

The eccentric boffin is obviously brainy, won't win the best-dressed man award (it's always a man; Carol Vorderman doesn't qualify!), and has an obsessive interest in strange and obscure things. He gets very excited, shouts a lot, waves his arms about and may well ride a bike! The evil professor is not nearly as lovable. He is a scientist who has gone off the rails and is power-mad. He threatens the planet in books and comics, on TV, films and computer games.

Stereotypes like these show the fear and fascination that science brings out in people. If you did a survey you might find scientists who are a bit like the stereotypes, but you would also discover that the kinds of people who study and work in science are as varied as doctors, lawyers, teachers or any other professional people.

Think carefully about these images and how they could affect your interest in science.

A scientist at work
by Natasha

Does studying science mean becoming a scientist?

In Chapter one, the point was made that people seem to confuse science the subject with science the career in a way that does not happen with other subjects. This observation was stated more strongly by a BBC science editor at a conference of the British Association for the Advancement of Science (BAAS) some years ago, but still rings true today:

> 'The problem starts at school. We do not teach students history or English and assume they will become historians or novelists; we do not teach French or German to equip students to become simultaneous translators; so why is science taught on the basis that students are going to become practising scientists?'

What do you think? Should science be part of everyone's general education, or is it something that is only important for people who want to become scientists?

Science is for all of us

Everyone must study some science at school until the age of 16, for 20% of school time as a part of the National Curriculum. There is a 'crisis of science' as not enough students are choosing physical science and engineering post-16 and at higher education level, which in turn leads to a shortage of science teachers.

Does this matter? Yes it does! We all need to make sense of the scientific developments taking place around us. The House of Commons Science and Technology Select Committee is concerned about the number of young people being 'turned off' science, and is trying to find ways of keeping them interested.

Following the Tomlinson report and a Government White Paper on 14-19 Education, the teaching of science up to GCSE level will change from 2006. There is a recognition that we all need to be scientifically literate to cope in today's technological society but that some will want to go further and prepare for a career that uses their science. A pilot scheme, 21st Century Science, developed since 2003 by the University of York in collaboration with Nuffield, the Royal Society and the scientific professional bodies, will result in most students doing two GCSEs in science instead of a 'double award'. The content will be much more up-to-date and relevant than previous science curricula. A range of options are being developed in 2005 which are designed to prepare pupils for different career routes. It is envisaged that those intent on a science career will be able to take 'additional science', giving them three science GCSEs. This process will eventually increase public awareness and understanding of science – especially among young people.

Stereotyping by teachers, parents, friends and careers advisers is blamed for turning many girls off science. Scientists' lack of visibility is also seen as a problem because there are few role models for people to follow. A lack of understanding about how science and technology links with jobs that are beneficial to society is also a concern. Body scanners, medicines, body implants, mobile phones and the internet are all examples of the products of science but it is often difficult for young people to see how the work of scientists fits into the development of such advances.

Financial incentives are attracting more science graduates into training as secondary science teachers. More good teachers should mean more enthused students, so the spiral could start going upward instead of downward.

Science and technology affect nearly all aspects of daily life, both at home and at work. As this dependence grows, a broad awareness of science and technology issues is essential for informed decision making.

Are we anti-science in Britain?

Based on purely anecdotal evidence of people responding to items on the news, there is genuine excitement at some of the recent rapid developments in science and technology. However, there is also widespread public anxiety about issues such as the uses and abuses of genetic modification, pollution, global warming, world energy resources and the possibilities of nuclear, chemical or biological terrorism. In Britain, science is often cast as the culprit, with scientists no longer trusted to find solutions. Many people today are suspicious of science and feel that technological progress is a threat to the environment. The exception seems to be medicine, where science is usually looked upon as our saviour (as long as cloning and cruelty to animals are not involved!).

Meanwhile, we all happily go on buying the latest digital gadgetry and wondering at the pictures sent back from outer space!

The status of science in Britain is reflected in the levels of pay some scientists receive. The organisation Campaign for Science and Engineering in the UK (CaSE) recently pressed for government and employers to 'improve the poor salaries and badly organised career structure for scientists to ensure the recruitment and retention of the best people into British science'. It can be difficult for scientists who are, on the whole, backroom workers to campaign for better pay. Biomedical scientists and pathologists, for example, are not well paid, but they don't have the high profile of nurses so have a harder time getting their case heard.

CaSE also attacked the lack of funding for school science laboratories and university science departments, and their campaign has met with some success. There is now more government funding going into these areas, so this situation should improve.

Britain has a distinguished history in science and should have a great future. British scientists have collected numerous Nobel prizes – the most recent, in 2003, being Sir Peter Mansfield for his work on the application of magnetic resonance imaging in physiology to investigate the organs of the body non-invasively, and Professor Anthony Leggett for studies of superfluidity phenomena in liquid helium. Just imagine being involved in such research. The scientists in our research laboratories and universities today are capable of following in the footsteps of their famous predecessors like Sir Isaac Newton and Charles Darwin (both finalists in the BBC's 2002 *Great Britons* poll) although commercial pressures may restrict 'pure' research to some extent.

Do scientists communicate well?

Some people feel that scientists have been partly to blame for their own bad press and poor public relations because of the kind of language they use and because the scientific community is seen as elitist.

Improving the communication skills of scientists is fundamental to making science more accessible to the public, but it is not just a one-way problem. All too often, non-scientists are quite happy to say – in fact, even to boast – that 'Science is just beyond me', or 'I couldn't understand a word they said', without making any effort to learn.

We think we can understand an artist, writer or composer because we can respond to their work and form an opinion about a painting or piece of music. With science it is not so easy, because the work often cannot be described in readily accessible and simplified terms. A certain level of scientific vocabulary and understanding is needed, and this cannot be picked up in ten minutes. Scientists even have this sort of communication problem when presenting their results to colleagues working in different fields.

Because of this difficulty in communicating, much of the excitement of scientific research and the creativity of developing ideas is lost to people outside science. Scientists may demonstrate their work with great zeal, but they are often trying to share the beauty of an idea or concept with a rather baffled audience.

Things are changing as public interest in science grows and more scientists learn to put across their knowledge and enthusiasm. Books like Stephen Hawking's *A Brief History of Time* and Dava Sobel's *Longitude* have been unexpected bestsellers in recent years. Bill Bryson, who is not a scientist and admits to 'growing up convinced that science was supremely dull' spent three years of his life learning about science. The result was *A Short History of Nearly Everything*, written to communicate the wonders of science without jargon or formulae. Another bestseller!

Scientists in the media

If you want to, you can hear and see a great number of scientists talking about science. Many young people listen to science programmes on the radio, such as *Material World*, and watch TV programmes like *Horizon, Rough Science* and *Best Inventions*. The Royal Society Christmas Lectures are an annual televised event, popular with children and adults alike. Many also read *New Scientist* and follow science articles in the press.

Good communicators and popularisers of science, such as Richard Dawkins and Steve Jones (the geneticists), Heather Couper (the astronomer), Ian Stewart (the mathematician) and Susan Greenfield (who talks inspiringly about how the brain functions), have gone some way to correct the stereotypes through science programmes on TV and radio. However, there is little opportunity to get to know scientists as media personalities in the same way as sports stars, politicians, actors, musicians and writers. Think about TV panel games, political discussions like *Question Time*, and chat shows: how many scientists appear on these programmes? A tiny minority, like Patrick Moore and Stephen Hawking, have become household names, but, in the main, science and scientists are kept in a world apart, not wholly of their own making.

Scientists at work
by Laura

Social and moral issues

There are many moral, social and political questions raised by developments in science. In 2005 the Royal Society published its views on the need to coordinate resources in the fight to combat infectious disease; the acidification of the oceans due to increasing atmospheric carbon dioxide; the effect that climate change will have on food crops; biological weapons and the importance of codes of conduct in preventing the misuse of scientific research. These are among the scientific topics that are most worrying in the public's mind.

Issues surrounding the use of stem cells to grow human tissue, how to deal with infectious diseases such as bird flu, how to counteract the possibility of terrorists using biological weapons and how to reach international consensus on action to reduce global warming all also raise ethical issues which lead to public discussion.

Should animals be used to test drugs? Should research into weapons of mass destruction be banned? Should food be irradiated to preserve it for longer? Should organs from specially reared pigs be used for xenotransplantation into humans? Should we build more nuclear power stations or invest in alternative energy? Should stem cell research be allowed?

These issues seem, to many people, to be much more interesting than the painstaking scientific work that leads to the stage where such questions need to be posed. It is very difficult to participate in discussions about the technical side of scientific developments unless you are very well up in the subject.

We want the answers

Another problem that seems to baffle non-scientists is why scientists don't know all the answers. School science often seems to deal with questions that are either right or wrong. There are facts to be learned and simple theories which can be tested by a laboratory experiment. It surely follows that there must be right and wrong answers to all scientific questions. Is the greenhouse effect getting worse? What is a safe dose of radiation? Is there a link between cancer and diet? Where and how did AIDS begin?

Scientists are heard giving different and contradictory opinions about topics such as these, and people say, 'Why can't they just give us the facts?' The trouble is that the 'facts' are often far from clear. Somehow the feeling is that scientists have failed if they can't give a straight answer, but there is no simple solution to many of these complex issues. The scientists are giving opinions based on their interpretation of the data available, and even the best data can rarely allow for all possible circumstances and eventualities.

How do we learn about science?

Controversial aspects of science are very newsworthy and often high on the political agenda. You and your friends are getting a lot of different messages about science and scientists from inside and outside school. This obviously has an effect on your subject preferences and career choices. Research on career choice shows that the stereotypes we discussed earlier are adopted very early on in primary school.

At primary school

Primary school children can be very enthusiastic about the sort of hands-on, basic science they are likely to be offered in the classroom. Curiosity comes naturally to them!

If you ask primary school children to draw a scientist, past surveys have shown that the majority will depict a man. Baldness, beards, spectacles and white coats will feature strongly. Scientists are usually depicted as white, even when drawn by black or Asian children. Backgrounds will almost always be indoor scenes, and often feature flasks, test tubes and beakers. Fewer show living things. Most primary school-age children have little or no personal knowledge of scientists, so these stereotypes are presumably drawn from books, comics, television and videos.

We commissioned our own small and unscientific survey of ten-year-olds' perceptions. A number of children did draw female scientists. The teacher assures us that the children were not briefed to do so; they just happened to be a group who were hot on equal opportunities. We have used some of their drawings to enliven the text in this chapter.

We also asked the children to write a few words about being a scientist. More said they would not like to be a scientist than said they would. Here are some of their impressions – with the original spelling:

'I would not like to be a scientist because I think it's two much work like studing the moon and space and stuff like that all the time.'

'I would like to be a scientist because you get to know a lot more about the world. I really like looking at things that are about space and dinosaur fossils.'

'I would not like to be a scientist because I find science a bit boring. Science is not my favourite subject, but I like looking and finding out facts about animals, nature, stars and the moon.'

'I would not like to be a scientist because you would have to get up early in the morning and get to work early, and I am not great with mornings. And I wouldn't be able to keep up with what I am meant to be doing.'

'I would not like to be a scientist because it is to much hard work, and to much investigating.'

'I would not like to be a scientist because you would have to risk your life because you would have to do dangerous stuff like visit the moon or go to different countries. You wouldn't get to see your family a lot.'

'I would not like to be a scientist because I would get confused and I wouldn't be able to keep up and I'll get lost in the work.'

A scientist at work by Krystle

'I'd like to be a scientist because I could come face to face with some of the rareist animals on the planet, maybe even dive down to the bottom of the seas and oceans and work on how fish can communicate, how the elephant is relaited to a rodent, to find a brand new bug.'

'I would not like to be a scientist because I think it would be quite boring and you would have to do quite hard stuff and its not my best subject. You would have to wear horrible clothes and you will get all hot in them.'

'I would like to be a scientist because I'll love to do some exciting experiments and explore places or animals that no one knows about.'

'I would not like to be a scientist because Science is not my faviorite thing to do. I would be scientist if I could not be a lawyer but really I am not very good at science anyway.'

'I would like to be a scientist because I like to mix potions and experimint what something would look like after they are put together and on TV I watch what they do so it looks interesting how they work.'

'If I was a scientist I would try to make a potion that works like gas to use for petrol so it lasts longer for long distance drivers.'

'I would not like to be a scientist because it is to much thinking of science. Science is to get every thing right so it works. Science is to do with Eelcitcy and Eelcitcy is dangerus.'

A scientist at work
by Leanna

'I would love to be a scientist. My opinion is "who wouldn't?" I think working on astronomy, Dinosaurs and Electricity is great. I would like to be an inventor. If you ask a friend of mine called Simon, he could tell you every single Dinosaur that lived! I would like to use all of the tools in Evolution.'

Sorry we don't have room to print all the children's contributions!

How do older schoolchildren see scientists?

'Some scientists do experiments. Others use their brains.'

That's a quote from an English schoolboy in a report of an international *Science and Scientists* project. The report* looks at the attitudes of over 9000 13-year-olds in 21 different countries. The study shows a greater enthusiasm for learning science and technology in the less-developed countries, possibly because education – particularly in this field – is still seen as a privilege, whereas in the richer countries education is seen as a duty imposed from above. The report concludes:

'The image of science and scientists is more positive among children in developing countries than in the rich countries. Children in the developing countries seem to be eager to learn science, and for them the scientists are the heroes. This is in marked contrast to at least a significant part of the children in the rich countries, who often express sceptical and negative attitudes and perceptions in their responses to several of the items. The notion of the crazy or mad scientist is often found in rich countries. Very few children in the rich countries envisage the scientist as a kind, human and helpful person, whereas this is often the image of scientists in developing countries.'

The images around you of science and scientists will have some effect on your choice of career and the subjects you decide to study after GCSE. But your opinion of science will also be influenced by your experience at school: one of the most significant factors for most people choosing science is an enthusiastic and interesting teacher. Unfortunately, there is still a serious shortage of specialist science teachers.

Another important factor is the way the science curriculum itself is designed. Critics say it is dull, outdated and needs to be interesting to pupils who have a broad range of different careers in mind. From 2006 the GCSE curriculum is changing to meet these objections and will be more relevant to the 21st century. Reformers say that these changes should encourage more students to take science at A level and beyond, while also providing scientific literacy for the majority who will just use their science to keep up with our modern technological society.

* *Sjoberg, S. (2002) Science for the children? Report from the Science and Scientists Project. Acta Didactia (1/2002). ISBN 82 90904 65 7.*

Study of at least two GCSEs in science, followed by relevant AS and A levels, will provide the knowledge and discipline necessary for young people to enter higher education in science and technology.

If you are at the year 9 'options' stage of your education, from 2006 you will be entitled to study at least two GCSEs in science. This may be through a GCSE science course that covers core science topics, and a second additional science GCSE course. If you want to make your career in an area which uses your knowledge of science, taking two science GCSEs is necessary. The old 'double science' system is being discontinued except for those studying for a double award in applied science.

It is advisable to keep abreast of science GCSE developments on such websites as The Royal Society, Nuffield and the Qualifications and Curriculum Agency and discuss it with your science teachers.

A scientist at work by Robert

Advanced level choice

It is at this level that the effects of subject preferences really begin to show. This is when you must narrow your subject choices to, usually, three or four subjects – occasionally five – in the present AS and A level system. This gives you some chance of keeping your options open by mixing sciences with other subjects before you decide on which two or three subjects you wish to take at A2 to gain the full A level. N.B. A levels in applied subjects, such as applied science, applied ICT and engineering, are work-related – helping you to develop the skills, knowledge and understanding needed for a particular vocational area.

Some A levels in applied subjects are available as 12-unit awards, as well as 6-unit and 3-unit awards. You need to check the attitude of individual higher education institutions to A levels in applied subjects, as many – especially the 'old' universities – ask for at least one traditional single science A level and/or maths A level for entry. Currently, however, universities are seeking to recruit their students from a more diverse range of backgrounds and with a broader range of qualifications than they have done in the past. This is known as 'the diversity agenda'.

Reasons for choosing certain subjects at Advanced level include:

■ getting good results at GCSE
■ finding the subject interesting and enjoyable
■ being encouraged by teachers who think you can pass at Advanced level
■ needing that particular subject for entry to a higher education course or career.

Enjoyment of a subject and good results at GCSE are the main factors for most people, but for those choosing science subjects, particularly physics and chemistry, the fact that they need the subjects for a course or career is more likely to be important. So the choice of science post-16 is affected by both subject preferences and career choice.

Alternatives to A level

An alternative route into either employment or higher education for school-leavers is to take an Advanced Apprenticeship with a science-based or engineering company. Many of these are for laboratory assistants learning science at work. In 2005, there were around 100,000 young people on Advanced Apprenticeships. Advanced Apprenticeships can lead to at least an NVQ (National Vocational Qualification) at level 3. Following this there is the possibility of progressing further, perhaps on to higher education. Reaching degree level by this route is a long and tortuous road, however.

Another possibility is to take BTEC National qualifications (equivalent to one, two or three A levels, depending on the number of units) in a scientific or engineering subject. This is a particularly good route for entry to a related Higher National Diploma course. These are highly vocational qualifications that relate to specific careers and develop a .practical 'can do' approach rather than a theoretical academic one.

A level entries in selected subjects 1999-2004

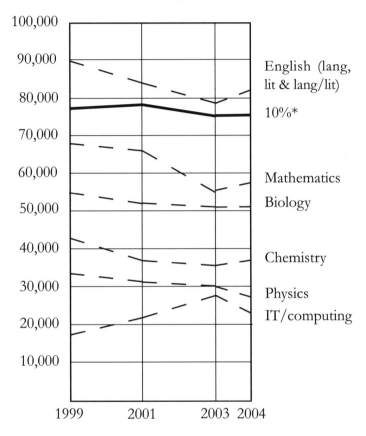

* The bold line on the graph represents 10% of the number of A level candidates for all subjects.

Source: Joint Council for General Qualifications

Are fewer people choosing sciences?

In recent years, when A level results have been published, one key story is that fewer students are taking A levels in maths and sciences. This in turn means a decline in students at HE level, and even the downsizing or closure of university maths and science departments. The graph opposite, on page 38, illustrates the trends.

Key points

■ IT and computing entries increased strongly up to 2003 and then declined by more than10%.

■ Physics has continued to decline but chemistry seems to have stabilised.

■ Maths appears to have recovered recently from a reduction that has been going on since 1999.

■ The graph also shows, interestingly, that English entries, which declined dramatically from 1999 have now begun to increase.

■ The number of biology entries, which had been increasing throughout the early 1990s, went into reverse after 1997 but has now stabilised.

■ When subjects such as maths or the sciences experience a reduction in numbers a shortage of people with advanced-level skills in those areas eventually emerges, which must mean better prospects for those who do gain such qualifications.

What is the chance of getting good grades?

The following data is based on 2004 A level results in maths, sciences and IT.

Percentages gaining each grade at A level in 2004

Grade	A	B	C	D	E	U
Biology	22	21	20	17	12	7
Chemistry	30	24	19	14	9	4
Physics	28	21	19	15	11	6
Maths	38	21	16	12	8	5
Computing/IT	14	19	22	22	15	7
All syllabuses	22	23	23	18	10	4

Source: Joint Council for General Qualifications

N.B. Figures may not add up to 100%, as they have been rounded up or down.

Key points

■ Results vary from year to year, and have tended to improve in recent years. The percentage of A grades in all of the above categories has increased continuously since 1998.

■ The proportion of students obtaining A or B grades in maths, physics and chemistry was higher than the average for all subjects. This contradicts the often quoted perception that 'science is harder' than other subjects.

■ These figures do not include those who gave up the course and did not attempt the exam.

Percentages gaining each grade at AS level in 2004

Grade	A	B	C	D	E	U
Biology	17	17	17	17	14	18
Chemistry	22	18	17	15	12	15
Physics	22	17	17	15	12	17
Maths	26	15	15	13	11	19
Computing/IT	12	16	19	18	15	20
All syllabuses	17	18	20	18	13	13

Source: Joint Council for General Qualifications

N.B. Figures may not add up to 100%, as they have been rounded up or down.

Key points

■ Maths gave the most successes but also the most failures.

■ As in the A level results, maths, physics and chemistry all have a higher percentage of A grades than the average for all subjects.

What happens in higher education?

Students choosing degree courses in sciences

The figures for those starting degree courses in the main science subjects in 1998, 2001 and 2004 are given below. The proportions of all students choosing each subject are shown by the percentages.

Students accepted onto degree courses in sciences 1998 – 2004

	1998		2001		2004	
	Number	%	Number	%	Number	%
Biological sciences	17,067	5.6	17,771	5.4	29,262	8.1
Physical sciences*	14,729	4.9	12,662	3.8	13,878	3.8
Physics	2997	1.0	2612	0.8	2671	0.7
Mathematical sciences/ Computing **	21,717	7.2	29,499	9.0	23,273	6.4
Engineering & technology	22,016	7.3	19,951	6.1	23,370	6.4
Combined sciences	6717	2.2	7802	2.4	5410	1.5
Total	302,683	28.2	329,218	27.5	362,985	4.9

Source: UCAS

* includes a range of subjects related to chemistry, physics, materials science and geology.

** maths/informatics prior to 2004.

Key points

■ Biological sciences are the most popular area of study in science and their popularity continues to grow. There was a 55% increase in the number of students accepted onto biological sciences degree courses in 2002 (from 17,771 to 27,657) and since then numbers have continued to rise.

■ The strong rise in numbers starting courses in maths and computing up to 2001 has halted following the bursting of the e-services bubble.

■ Combined science entries have decreased.

■ Medicine, dentisty and veterinary science (not shown in the table) continue to attract applicants with strong science qualifications. Demand for places exceeds supply and many of these courses have introduced an additional entrance exam on top of A levels. Many of the rejected students find their way onto other science-related courses. Some students first complete a degree in a related life science and then join a special four-year graduate degree course leading to qualification as a medical doctor. Places in medical schools have been expanding recently in an attempt to meet the demands of the profession, in which there is a shortage of doctors. The morality of recruiting doctors from developing countries, where there is an even greater shortage of medical staff, is being challenged.

■ The numbers doing Higher National Diploma courses in sciences are very small in comparison with the numbers on degree courses and have declined since the introduction of foundation degrees. 14,559 students registered for these courses in 2004 compared with 28,823 in 2001.

■ Foundation degrees were first offered in 2001 when 4,000 students registered. By 2004 this number had risen to 24,000 and there are over 80 different foundation degrees now available in science and mathematics.

Getting into higher education

The ratio of applicants to places in higher education is not straightforward to calculate because each applicant can choose up to six different courses. In general, there are many fewer applicants per place for science courses than for arts, social science or business studies. However, this does not necessarily mean that the quality of the applicants is lower. Physics, for example, does not attract as many applicants as other subjects, but those who do apply tend to have high A level grades. Medical and veterinary courses are known to be very competitive, so most of the applicants are expected to achieve high grades. Some engineering courses have trouble recruiting enough students, so may accept lower grades. At some universities they offer extra maths and physics tuition to students who are not quite ready for degree-level study. There is more information in Chapter four about the requirements for courses in higher education.

A scientist at work by Stephen

Are science students different?

There are more similarities between students than there are obvious differences. Contrary to some expectations, you will be able to find history students who say that they have technical minds and dislike working with people. You will equally find science students who describe themselves as imaginative and having a broad outlook on life. And people who are good at a subject tend not to find their courses difficult. So pushing yourself into subject choices by trying to match yourself to the perceived qualities of a typical student is not likely to be productive. It is much better to follow your own abilities and interests.

What about the career aspects?

First employment figures for graduates get a lot of publicity. Lots of anecdotal information feeds back into the schools and colleges where you and your friends are making subject choices and university applications. We hope we have already destroyed the stereotype of the scientist with limited career choices. Science, mathematics and technology graduates fare pretty well on the jobs market overall. They are less likely to be unemployed than are arts and humanities graduates, and average earnings are higher for science graduates than for all graduates (although, interestingly, not for jobs which specifically require science degrees). See Chapters five and eight for details of graduate careers and employment statistics.

Science graduates who opt to do a PhD as a three-year full-time higher degree by research, leading to the title Doctor of Philosophy (see Chapter six for more details) face another three years on a very low income. However, most feel that it is well worth it. Starting salaries are around £2000 more for PhD-holders than for an average first-degree graduate (although this, of course, will vary from individual to individual, depending on factors such as the relevance of the PhD to the job in question, for example).

Science graduates sometimes feel that their pay levels do not reflect the contribution they make. The ones who go into careers such as finance, patent work or management consulting or those who become actuaries after graduating invariably enjoy much higher starting salaries than scientists in industry, healthcare or in the academic world, though their hours of work may be longer.

A science degree does not guarantee a job, but it can give you a clear advantage by opening up a broader range of careers than an arts degree. Degree subjects like accountancy or law may sound much safer, but science will give you more flexibility in your career plans and a science degree can be a stepping stone into both of these careers. As you will see later in this book, science graduates can leave their options open and choose later from areas of work in both science-related and non-scientific disciplines. The important thing is to gather as much information as you can before making your decision.

There are skills shortages in science and technology (as confirmed by Sir Gareth Robert's government-commissioned review into the supply of science and engineering skills in the UK, published in 2002). A major result of the Roberts review has been an increase in the opportunities that are made available for science students to develop a whole range of transferable skills, such as report writing, technical presenting, negotiating, interviewing and many more.

Science awareness is growing

In the UK

The Government is aware of the shortage of science and technology graduates, and how much of that is due to the poor image of science. *Strategic Science Provision in English Universities* – a report published by the House of Commons Science and Technology Committee in 2005 – rehearses the difficulties and searches for solutions. Funding for these areas of higher education – especially for research – has recently been increased, and various bodies (*see* Campaigns and initiatives – page 212) are trying to improve the image and attractiveness of a science education to avoid skill shortages in the future. There is now more science in primary schools and prospective primary teachers must have science GCSE at grades A*-C. Some primary and most secondary schools are involved in practical science and technology projects which are supported by employers and industrial organisations.

There are also many science fairs and exhibitions, aimed at both children and adults, that try to convey the excitement and wonder of science to the public. Activities like these and centres like The Science Museum in London, Techniquest in Cardiff, The Magna Science Adventure Centre in Rotherham and @Bristol are much more hands-on than science museums used to be. They involve visitors of all ages in the experience of science. There are other science lectures and events run by organisations such as the Royal Society and the separate science institutions and societies. Ask your science teacher for more information, or visit some of the websites listed later in this book.

Other initiatives are aimed at science teachers rather than students, and there are schemes where teachers can spend time in industry working with local companies to develop projects for their schools.

Science in other countries

Science has a superior status in many other countries. Its lower status in this country is sometimes blamed on the traditional English public school bias toward the classics and humanities. Even families which made their fortunes through advances in technology in the industrial revolution wanted their offspring to have this sort of classical education.

Perhaps because science was not a compulsory subject up to the age of 16 until quite recently, the UK adult population's understanding of science does not compare well with that in many developed countries in Europe and Asia. Large UK companies are supporting school science programmes because of industry's worries about the low level of scientific understanding in their workforce.

A new image

The initiatives mentioned above and the concerns that drive them should lead to changes in perceptions of science and scientists. With all young people now studying some science at school, the standard of scientific knowledge is improving. This should mean more questioning of the stereotypes and more positive feelings about science and scientists, although pupils may still see science as a difficult subject.

Science graduates are increasingly going into other work such as accountancy, where graduates are traditionally better represented in top management. As a result, in time, there will be more science graduates in top jobs in industry and government. There is a specialist fast-track scheme for science and engineering graduates in the Civil Service – or they can choose the generalist scheme instead.

The science faculties in universities are becoming more aware of the importance of communication skills for scientists. Higher education institutions now realise the value placed by employers on high standards of communication and other key skills, especially teamwork and commercial awareness, whatever the degree subject.

Links with the rest of Europe, where science has greater prestige, are being strengthened. Programmes, such as Socrates-Erasmus and Leonardo, foster the exchange of scientific personnel and students between European countries. Increased contact between governments and through other European agencies should help to increase the status of British scientists. Many UK qualifications are now recognised and accepted throughout the EU.

The number of women in science and science-related jobs is gradually increasing, so there are more role models for younger women. The fact that there are more women scientists and science teachers will help both sexes to deal with some of the damaging stereotypes. Awareness of equal opportunities issues in science is improving at school and in science careers.

Women have always been well represented in the media, and there are many more opportunities now in science publishing, journalism and the other media. The BBC, for instance, has several women science correspondents. Sue Watts – a physics graduate, and science correspondent for the *Tonight* programme – played a key role in the recent Hutton enquiry. These women are in a position to have a good influence and act as role models for young women beginning their careers.

Summary

There are many good reasons for examining the images of science and scientists more closely, rather than allowing the stereotypes to limit your choices and your career aspirations. Things are changing and will continue to change.

■ Developments in science lead to advances in technology. Understanding these developments will enable you to deal with the changes that are coming and their consequences. A scientific education will allow you to take a part in shaping the future.

■ There is a shortage of science, engineering and technology graduates, perhaps because of a lack of awareness of the range of jobs open to science graduates.

■ The assumption that if you are interested in science you will have to become a research scientist is wrong. Scientific knowledge has a multitude of uses.

■ Despite general public interest in issues raised by developments in science, scientific understanding is still not widely seen as an important part of our culture. Efforts are being made to interest the general public and increase science awareness in many different ways.

■ The influence and prominence of scientists will change as more young science graduates move into a wider range of careers.

■ Negative stereotypes of scientists should disappear, as the number of science graduates in the general population increases and scientific knowledge improves generally.

Chapter three
Women and men in science

This chapter covers:

- sexual stereotypes of science and scientists

- male and female subject choices at A level or the equivalent, and in higher education

- influences on girls and boys making subject choices

- women at work/discrimination

- how girls can get support when choosing science subjects and scientific careers.

In Chapter two one factor that cropped up was gender – the male stereotype of a scientist. This chapter considers the problem in more detail and asks why many girls are turned off science. It also looks at the data on female and male subject choices at each stage of education, and speculates as to why the differences arise. This is a topic everyone has views on, so be prepared to argue and disagree. It is important to understand the influence of gender: how it affects the way you think about science and the decisions you make about your subjects and career.

But first ... a test

Spot the female scientists!

Hint: there is one woman on each horizontal row.

(Answers on page 68)

I Newton	C Darwin	D Hodgkin
J Watson	L Pauling	B McClintock
M Curie	A Einstein	F Crick
S Hawking	R Franklin	F Sanger
A Fleming	C Herschel	Frankenstein

How did you do? Can you think of any other women scientists? It's not surprising if you find it difficult because women scientists are still outnumbered by men today and there were even fewer in the past.

Engineering and construction, both areas with great skills shortages, attract even fewer women than science.

Although 57% of graduates are women, only 23% of physics graduates and 22% of information technology graduates are female. In mechanical and electrical engineering the figures are even lower, with 9% and 11% respectively. These figures have risen significantly in recent years but there is still some way to go. Yet in biology, women outnumber men by almost two to one, while in environmental science and chemistry the gender balance is almost equal. There is clearly a lot of sexual stereotyping going on. Evidence given to the House of Commons Science and Technology Committee in 2004 by Mori, the market research organisation, found that in 2001 only 1% of girls wanted to be engineers. Girls perceived engineering as 'a boring occupation, and one which required work in a dirty environment'. The reality is, of course, very different but few girls have access to places where electronic or mechanical engineers work. By contrast, biological sciences appear to be more attractive to women, being seen as more caring and in tune with people's needs.

A European Commission report in 2005, *Women and Science; excellence and innovation – Gender equality in Science* concluded that the number of women in top jobs in science is growing, but only slowly. While 44% of students in science and technology around Europe are female, only 14% of top academics are women. Only 4.5% of the fellows of the Royal Society are female but of those scientists elected to the fellowship over the last 5 years 10.3% are women. Just 9.5% of science professors are female.

There are numerous organisations working to encourage more girls to take science, engineering and technology (SET) subjects beyond GCSE, and pursue SET careers. Examples of these include WISE – the Women into Science and Engineering Campaign, WES – the Women's Engineering Society, the Association of Women in Science and Engineering, the Athena Project, the European Association for Women in Science Engineering and Technology and many more. Relevant websites are listed in the 'useful addresses' section on page 211.

On biology degree courses there are twice as many women as men, yet no organisations are specifically endeavouring to attract men into the subject. Professional bodies such as the Institute of Biology, the Biochemical Society and the Institute of Biomedical Science offer plenty of information, however, to those attracted to the biological sciences, whether female or male.

A woman's place

The earliest records of women in technology go back to ancient Egypt. Despite that, historically, women have not been expected to play an active role in science. Even when they did they were often not given credit for their work. One of the most widely read early medical texts in Europe was written by an Italian woman called Trotula in the 11th century. She was one of a group of medical women known as the 'ladies of Salerno', but for centuries it was assumed that her work was written by a man. It also now seems that Pythagoras' wife had a lot to do with his writings on the Golden Mean. In more recent times many people were outraged that Rosalind Franklin was not properly recognised for her contribution to the understanding of DNA. Similarly, Jocelyn Bell Burnell missed out on a share of the Nobel Prize for the discovery of pulsars.

Some women have got recognition, however. Ada Lovelace, daughter of Lord Byron, has been called 'the world's first computer programmer' for her work with Charles Babbage's 'thinking machine' in the mid-19th century, and has been featured on Microsoft's watermark. Marie Curie won two Nobel prizes and later her daughter Irene won one for physics. When Barbara McClintock suggested that genes could 'jump around' on a chromosome, the members of the American National Academy of Sciences were less than enthusiastic. She says, 'They thought I was crazy, absolutely mad!' But she was right and won a Nobel prize in 1983.

A man's field?

The pursuit of science is often portrayed as competitive rather than collaborative, with the outcome being to control nature rather than to understand and work with the natural world. The language used in the media to portray science often has a 'masculine' sound to it – conquering, controlling, probing to the depths, overcoming, a race against nature, unlocking the secrets of mother nature, penetrating the secrets of the universe!

Not all science graduates become research scientists, however, and there are many other opportunities for people qualified in science. These jobs require all sorts of other qualities and skills and offer rewarding prospects, but many girls do not get to the starting post because they have already turned away from science. Creativity, intuition, communication and teamwork are all-important attributes for scientists, and often assumed to be feminine traits! Neuroscientist Baroness Susan Greenfield, one of the UK's most successful women scientists today, suggests in an interview in the *Guardian* newspaper one aspect of science that girls should be made more aware of.

'Contrary to popular belief, science is, I believe, as creative as writing a novel or a symphony: no two people will do it in the same way.'

Boys too are influenced by the kind of images and stereotypes discussed in Chapter two. Perhaps some choose science because it seems expected of them, when they might prefer something different. Some, like Bob Simpson (profile page 117), start out wanting to be a vet, a doctor or a dentist but find the competition too severe.

So where do these perceptions of science and scientists start?

Gender in education

A higher proportion of female than male candidates achieve grades A*-C in GCSE single and double science awards, but at A level (in 2004), girls accounted for only 22% of physics candidates and 12% of computing candidates. In biology A level, however, 60% of the candidates were girls, while in chemistry the numbers of girls and boys were about equal. Why is this?

What happens in education to influence both girls and boys in career and subject choices? And what has been happening in the past to discourage girls from achieving their potential as scientists?

Back to primary school

In Chapter two, there are some pictures of scientists drawn by ten-year-old children. These are actually atypical, as they do show some female scientists (drawn by girls, of course!). Previous surveys have shown that boys and girls pick up stereotypes of male, bald and/or bearded, bespectacled scientists early in their primary school career. As, because of the gender imbalance in primary-school teaching, most primary science is taught by women, we can only conclude that children's films, comics, computer games and so on help to establish this stereotype.

Secondary school

At GCSE, there is no scope for boys and girls to make different choices because the National Curriculum requires everyone to do science. The proportions of boys and girls getting higher grade GCSE passes in individual sciences and maths are not greatly different, although the girls have a slight edge.

In English language, however, the gap is much wider, with boys' results at GCSE way behind the girls'. This gets much less publicity, but it may also have a bearing on boys' subject choices. Some may opt for science because they are less confident in the language skills needed for subjects that require more essay writing.

Both boys and girls seem to make up their minds about studying science early on in secondary school. Unfortunately, girls are more easily put off. If they find the subject becoming difficult they are more likely to conclude that it is too hard for them and lose interest. Boys who have difficulty with science and maths tend to see themselves as lazy, whereas girls who have problems may see themselves as stupid.

Some likely reasons given for the number of girls who drop out of science post-16 are:

- girls are often alienated by the impersonal and value-free aspect of science
- many girls have never met a female engineer
- girls want to work in a socially supportive environment, and don't see scientific jobs as fulfilling that need.

A lot of girls have a suitable science base at GCSE but few of them choose to study the subjects beyond GCSE. Many of these girls have better results than some of the boys who do continue with sciences.

It may be the way science is taught in schools that puts girls off. One view is that science experiments are too abstract: they are not set in a context which relates to real life and real problems, and so fail to attract the interest of many girls. It will be interesting to see what effect – if any – the increase in specialist technology schools and colleges has on gender balance.

What happens in your school? Do you think boys and girls have different attitudes to science, maths and computing? Do you find girls more attracted to biology and boys to physics or computing? It is known that girls are more likely to continue studying science and maths in a single-sex school, and boys are more likely to choose music and arts in boys-only schools. So peer group pressure from both sexes seems to influence both boys and girls in making their choices.

A visit to any school's computer room in the lunch hour will confirm the gender gap. The content of computer games does not appeal to girls as much as it does to boys. This alienates many girls and undermines their confidence in the use of computers for more serious purposes.

What happens at AS and A level?

Because science A levels are required for entry to virtually all science, engineering and medical degree courses (see Chapter four for details), the choices you make at this stage are crucial.

Percentages of boys and girls taking A and AS levels in science subjects in 2004

	AS		A	
	M	**F**	**M**	**F**
Biology	40	60	40	60
Chemistry	50	50	49	51
Physics	75	25	78	22
Mathematics	60	40	61	39
Computing/IT	88	12	88	12

Source: Joint Council for General Qualifications

N.B. Girls make up 54% of the total A level and AS level candidates for the year shown, across the whole spectrum of subjects.

As you can see from the chart, a lot more girls choose biology, which may be advantageous for many of the so-called 'caring' careers in medicine, veterinary science, etc. If you do choose biology it is a good idea to take chemistry too. Chemistry A level is essential for entry into medical school and important if you want to study biology at university. Perhaps that is why chemistry attracts both sexes equally. It is in physics and computing that girls are so poorly represented. Girls have deserted computing and IT in recent years. While 23% of the candidates for A level computing were female in 2001, by 2004 that figure had plummeted to just 12%. Meanwhile the percentage of girls taking A level physics remains unchanged at 22%. Yet physics is a subject that opens up a huge range of career options in science and engineering, and girls are just as capable as boys at the subject.

What about degree courses?

Proportions of men and women accepted onto science degree courses in 2004

Subject group	Women (%)	Men (%)
Maths	38	62
Physics	17	83
Chemistry	41	59
Biological sciences	62	38
Computer science	14	86
Engineering & technology	18	82
All subjects	54	46

Source: UCAS

In the population as a whole there are slightly more teenage boys than girls but more girls than boys go to university. 54% of those starting university courses in 2004 were girls.

Women are much more attracted to undergraduate courses in the biological sciences than men, though in 2004 38% of those starting biological science courses were men, so men have been catching up. Although roughly equal numbers of boys and girls take chemistry at A level, and both sexes get good results, a slightly smaller proportion of females go on to study a degree in chemistry and the trend is downwards by 2 percentage points in the last three years. Girls are more interested in maths than they were.

No-one knows why so few girls have an interest in computing, though the reasons rehearsed earlier in this chapter are a part of the answer. Again the participation of women in computer science degrees has declined by 6% in the last three years. Certainly employers in the IT sector desperately need more women on their staff and are perplexed about how to attract them.

There has been a steady increase in the proportion of females studying engineering and physics over the last few years, though it is incremental rather than a quantum leap.

There are many other degree courses attracting students with science A levels. Women tend to favour degree courses allied to medicine, veterinary science, environmental science and food science. Although these are not the so called 'hard sciences', they are far from soft options in terms of A level grades and competition for places.

Choosing the right place

When choosing a degree course you have many things to consider: the syllabus, the university or college facilities, and the social and educational environments and the location – town or country. There may also be major differences in approach between courses. Chapter four will help you to look at these issues.

There is another significant factor that could influence your choice: the ratio of women to men on the course. Girls applying for a course in engineering or physics, for example, can expect to be in a small minority, while in the biological sciences the minority is male. It is very important to choose your course and university carefully: there is a big difference in terms of ratios (and attitudes) between courses. Find out what the present gender ratios are on courses you are considering and try to talk to students who are already there. Ask if there are any women lecturers.

For boys, too, there will be gender considerations. Some may prefer to be on a course where the students are predominantly male, while most probably feel happier with a more even gender balance.

Postgraduate and beyond

In postgraduate education there is a similar pattern. While 46% of all PhDs awarded to UK-domiciled students in 2003 were given to women, 59% of PhDs in the biological and biomedical sciences were women, but only 28% of those in the physical sciences and engineering (*What Do PhD Graduates Do?* published by UK Grad).

Attempts are being made to attract and retain more women in academic life and these efforts appear to be meeting considerable success. One reason given for women leaving academia is that most full-time academic posts go to people in their mid-thirties – which can conflict with a woman's wish to have a family. By that stage, academic staff are expected to have some research materials published. Legislation coming into force in 2006, outlawing ageism in recruitment, should have a positive effect there. Another problem is the difficulty of keeping up with progress in science and technology during a career break. The Athena Project was set up to focus on the unacceptable wastage of the skills and talents of women academics in science, engineering and technology (SET) in higher education.

The gap

So, as people go through the education system from GCSE, to A level, to university and then on to postgraduate study and academic research, females have in the past been outnumbered by males in the physical sciences and engineering. Why did this happen?

There are all sorts of theories put forward to explain this phenomenon. Is it, for instance, something to do with a difference in the 'innate abilities' of males and females? Physics requires more maths than biology does and needs higher 'spatial' ability: that is, the ability to deal with three dimensions and relationships in space. (These differences are explored in the book *Why men don't listen and women can't read maps* published by Comet Publishing.) While there is an element of truth in this, the differences in spatial ability between males and females found in whole population studies are very slight. So it does not explain the huge discrepancy in the numbers of males and females choosing science subjects such as physics.

In other words, there are lots of girls choosing not to study maths and science, even though their mathematical and spatial abilities are considerably higher than many boys who do choose the subjects. Modern biology requires a high level of spatial ability in order to understand molecular structures, and women deal with it just as well as men.

Figures also show that women make fewer grant applications for scientific research, and for smaller amounts, which seems to show a continuing lack of confidence on their part in their academic status.

Career perceptions

Another important factor influencing the choices that girls make is their perception of the careers that science subjects lead on to. The point was made earlier that there is an expectation that someone studying science will become 'a scientist'.

The perception of the biological sciences is that they lead to careers in healthcare or the environment: jobs that are about helping people and looking after the natural world. Careers in these areas seem to girls, and to many boys, to be more useful and socially acceptable when compared with physical sciences, which have perceived links to weapons of war and causes of pollution.

It is unfortunate that many girls rule certain subjects out without really considering the potential career development possibilities. Their decisions are often based on a limited view of the context in which these subjects are useful. Physics, for example, has many applications in communications, the media, health (e.g. optics, cancer diagnosis and treatment), the development of new materials, computers and the environment. Physicists are involved, with other scientists and mathematicians, in the bid to explain and tackle problems like the greenhouse effect and global warming. Similarly, chemistry is useful for careers in healthcare, textiles, food technology and cosmetics – as well as the jobs in chemical engineering, oil refining, brewing, etc, which may be seen as 'macho'.

Once again, appearances can be deceptive. Graduates in the physical sciences are often regarded by employers to be highly numerate and possessing good analytical skills, so they can be found in management consulting, finance, IT, market research and many other areas of work, as well as in jobs that can be described as scientific or technical. It will pay you to find out more before you make a decision.

Sally Sunderland

Sally is a good example of a woman who has succeeded in what many people would still consider as 'a man's world' – civil engineering and construction.

Career profile

Job title: site agent

Employer: Hochtief (UK) Construction

A levels: maths (pure and applied), physics, biology

Degree: civil engineering HND and degree

University: Portsmouth

'There was no doubt about one of the A levels I would take: I loved maths. The other two subjects I took to make up the numbers. I felt that they would give me more of an option in deciding what I wanted to do.

In terms of career ambition, I started off wanting to work on an oil rig, then wanted to go into boat building and finally settled on civil engineering. Why? In the UCAS handbook it sounded exciting; I didn't like the thought of being office-bound and I really wanted to work outside.

My first choice for higher education was Southampton, but I didn't do well enough in my A levels. Portsmouth offered me the chance to do an HND (instead of the degree I wanted to do). I spent two years on the HND course and then transferred to the second year of the degree course. I loved it. I did two more years straight through and graduated in 1990.

The subjects on the course included fluid mechanics, structural analysis, geotechnics and surveying. Assessment was by exams at the end of each year, together with marks from projects. Notably, the design project sticks in my mind.

I spent the summers during my degree course working on a construction site – a road bypass – as a junior engineer for Rush and Tompkins. The experience was invaluable and I learnt a lot about working with people, the basics of engineering and discipline!

I joined Hochtief (UK) Construction as a junior engineer after graduating. I was based on site and spent years travelling up and down the country. I became a chartered engineer through the Institution of Civil Engineers in 1995. Part of my progression to become chartered involved working for a year in a design office in London, which I spent with Halcrow in their tunnelling department. I progressed through the ranks to section engineer in 1996 when I was sent to work on a contract in Kent, Thanet Way Dualling, to look after a number of structures – the main one being a 300-metre-long cut-and-cover tunnel.

In 1997, I was given my first real job as a site agent, replacing a railway bridge over the River Exe. It involved demolition and rolling the new structure into place. It went well. I then moved on as site agent to another railway bridge in Chippenham. This was more complex and involved giving up my Christmas to slide a new bridge under the rail tracks!

Following that, I spent time at Bristol Parkway Railway Station, where we had several contracts. Then in 2000 I left Hochtief to spend a year with an earthworks company.

I returned to Hochtief in 2001 and am currently the site agent to a £26 million scheme at Paddington Station. It's an exciting job. We have lifted an existing bridge 10 metres up in the air and are launching a new bridge underneath. This is definitely the highlight of my career so far. It is due to be completed in 2006 and is on time and within budget.

I love working on site. I strive to be successful in what I do and I would like to continue that way. From the experience I've gained, I would advise anyone to study science and maths in preparation for an engineering course. In engineering you meet such a wide range of people and have a varied career. You certainly can't get bored!'

Women at work

■ Women outnumber men as laboratory technicians.

■ Among professional engineers there are three grades. 3.2% of chartered engineers (the top professional grade), 1% of incorporated engineers and 1.2% of engineering technicians are female. However, among new entrants to the profession the number of females is growing at the rate of 6% per year.

■ Nearly one-third of all female employees in the engineering industry are operators or assemblers.

Employers are very aware of the need to recruit and retain highly skilled women as well as men in science and technology, when there is a shortage of graduates in these fields.

Women today are going into a much wider range of jobs. Changes in attitudes and lifestyles mean that more young graduate mothers are choosing to stay on in their careers. Employers are now obliged to seriously consider any request for flexible working arrangements from parents, and to give good reasons for turning a request down. Career patterns are constantly shifting and developments will benefit many women graduates.

Sadly, many girls are unaware of career opportunities for scientists in areas like patent work, information science, clinical research, technical marketing, science journalism and publishing, and health and safety. Some become discouraged and drop science early on in school.

Other areas where women with a science education and good communication skills are making an invaluable contribution are education and public understanding of science issues. Although they are still in a minority, women are moving into politics and the higher echelons of the administrative Civil Service, where there is a crying need for a greater understanding of science and science issues.

In industry, scientists are being employed increasingly in teams of multidisciplinary specialists. This is the type of cooperative working practice which many women and men prefer to the more hierarchical structure of the traditional company.

Finally, the transferable skills from a science degree, such as numeracy, logical and systematic problem solving, and work planning, can be very powerful tools when combined with expertise in areas like communications that are often regarded as 'feminine skills'. The administration of science, for instance, is an increasingly important field, as funding has to be specifically targeted and resources carefully managed. People employed in research science have to explain precisely what they are trying to do and why, in order to convince grant-awarding bodies of the importance of their work; so women who write and communicate well have the edge.

Discrimination

It is one thing to choose a science career, but quite another to succeed and advance within it. Sexual discrimination and sexual harassment are illegal. Unfortunately, discrimination occurs in all types of work, but it can sometimes be particularly difficult for a woman going into a company or a research group dominated by men who are suspicious of, or just unused to, women graduates. Clearly, some women can deal with this situation much better than others, but it is a very important factor to be aware of when considering a job, for exactly the same reasons as when choosing a degree course.

Recent reports have suggested that any discrimination is likely to be of an institutionalised kind. In other words, it is the organisational structure and traditional career progression routes that discriminate against women, rather than individual attitudes. In some organisations there can be a 'laddish culture' where women feel isolated and at a disadvantage.

Women's careers are traditionally more likely to be affected by having a family than men's are. This may be why more female graduates choose teaching as a career, either straight after university or later on. It might also explain why some women settle for posts as science technicians rather than going further. With the rapid pace of technological developments there is obvious concern that any career break could result in a woman in a science-oriented career feeling out of touch very quickly. Nevertheless, employers are required to give mothers maternity leave and keep their jobs open for them until they return. Those women who take many years out of science, however, can feel that it is difficult to catch up with the pace of change. We've already talked about these problems in relation to an academic career.

These pressures occur in most professional jobs but it is particularly important for graduate research scientists to establish themselves when they are young. They must be prepared to work long and anti-social hours in the lab at a time when they may have very young families, or when they want to start a family.

The report, *Women Physicists Speak*, emphasised that women need to be more assertive when applying for jobs and for research funding, as well as in the workplace generally, if discrimination is to end. Established women scientists and engineers should act as long-term mentors to younger women.

How will the situation change?

The good news is that things are changing. The European Commission's 2005 report *Women in Science: Excellence and Innovation – Gender Equality in Science* notes that gender gaps in education and employment are reducing. Throughout Europe women (58%) outnumber men in education. 41% of PhD graduates throughout Europe are now women, and the employment rates for women have been increasing. However, women still earn 16% less than men despite government action to address this issue – it is not legal to offer significantly different pay to two people in the same job, and mechanisms have been introduced to make pay more transparent. More needs to be done, the report says, to address men on gender issues in a way that will 'promote a cultural change within the workplace in support of gender equality'. In the past, campaigns to address gender issues have been exclusively targeted on women.

A key obstacle to women's participation in employment is the role of women within the family and the need to access affordable childcare. While 30% of women in the workforce are in part-time jobs, only 7% of men work part-time. The UK government has moved in recent years to improve the rights of part-time workers so that they are equal to those of full-timers. The Government has also made significant improvements in the availability of affordable childcare and in financial arrangements to make this easier. All of these measures are helping to remove disincentives for women to enter a science career, and slowly but surely closing the 'gender gap'.

The biological sciences, where women are in the majority, have recently seen more women in higher academic jobs and in jobs in the growing biotechnology industry.

But even in this field, only 9% of professors are women. The Biotechnology and Biological Sciences Research Council recently received a Business in the Community Gold Standard 'Opportunity Award' for sex equality. Among the research scientists it employs at its laboratories 264 are female and 236 are male. Among its support staff in engineering, IT and administration 373 are women and 310 are men.

There is more pressure to give active encouragement to all young people who want to do science, but particularly to girls. Your friends and classmates also have a strong influence on you, and the pressure on girls to give up science doesn't come from the opposite sex! There are lots of examples of girls helping each other too. When women undergraduates find themselves outnumbered on university courses they often work together in practical classes and in tutorials to provide mutual support.

In response to concerns about young people not being interested in science, there is now a lot more imaginative teaching material around. There's a lot of interactive material on websites, too. Resources are now much more carefully scrutinised for gender bias and teachers are more aware of the danger of stereotyping.

As the global economy and European community become more part of our lives, the influence from other countries where women have a stronger position in science and technology is increasing.

Support for women

As well as informal help from like-minded friends, and the strong support many girls get from their families and teachers, there are many women's groups dedicated to helping women choose and pursue a career in science. Women In Science and Engineering (WISE) is a national campaign with local branches which provides courses and speakers. WISE publishes a *Directory of Initiatives*, such as awards, sponsorship, courses, visits, and family-friendly employment policies. Most of the professional and academic bodies also have women's sections. All these groups offer advice and support either to individuals or to schools. In fact, there are around 70 organisations specifically to help women in science, engineering and technology (some of them are listed towards the end of this book). The Greenfield report suggests they should be consolidated!

Every year universities and science organisations run short 'taster' courses, lasting up to one week, for school students who are potential science and technology undergraduates.

The UK Resource Centre for Women in Science, Engineering and Technology, funded by the Department for Trade and Industry (DTI), has a number of joint campaigns with industry to attract more women into SET employment, and to encourage some of the thousands of women scientists who have left the field to return.

Science needs more women

- Science needs more women, just as much as women need the career opportunities that a science degree can offer.

- Girls can do as well as – or better than – boys at AS and A level and equivalent; they just need the confidence and encouragement.

- If you are not sure about science at HE level or as a career, choose AS and A levels that keep your options open for as long as possible: it's very hard to go back after you've dropped science.

- A science degree does not just lead into a laboratory: there are lots of other careers open to science graduates.

- There are lots of interesting women science and technology graduates like the ones in the profiles in this book. Try to meet and talk to some.

- There are many organisations that can help and give you support, from your local Connexions and university careers service to national organisations like WISE. Make good use of them.

In summary

- Many girls opt out of science in spirit long before they reach their GCSE exams. They are influenced by peer group pressure and easily discouraged if they find the subjects difficult. They often decide against science before they are aware of the wide variety of careers that science qualifications can offer.

- Women seem to prefer biology to physics and tend to choose subjects where they can see applications in contexts such as health or the environment.

- The practicalities of family life still seem to have a strong influence, but this is changing as more young women graduates combine a career with having children, and employers introduce more flexible working practices for their staff.

- There are many welcome changes ahead; as career structures are altered, as more women gradually become established in science-based careers, and as more international influences reach men and women in Britain. Things would change faster if there were more young women science, engineering and technology graduates around to help!

Spot the female scientist! (Answers)

Dorothy Hodgkin (1910-94) – crystallographer who discovered the structure of vitamin B12. The *Daily Mail* reported her Nobel prize victory in 1964 as 'British Wife wins Nobel Prize'.

Barbara McClintock (1902-92) – geneticist who won the 1983 Nobel prize for Physiology and Medicine.

Marie Curie (1867-1934) – physicist who discovered radioactivity and won two Nobel prizes.

Rosalind Franklin (1920-58) – chemist and crystallographer who made a major contribution to the discovery of DNA.

Caroline Herschel (1750-1848) – astronomer and mathematician.

Chapter four
Choosing science courses in higher education

This chapter covers:

- the types of higher education courses available
- how you can keep open a range of options
- the importance of mathematics

- subject ideas and some of the criteria you might employ in choosing a science degree subject
- grades and UCAS tariff points
- ways of combining advanced level subjects
- changing track
- where to go for further information and advice.

Choosing the right type of course

Andy Malone (page 182) put a lot of thought into his choice of degree course ...

'In choosing a university degree I looked for a course in physics that gave me the flexibility to also study geology. In the end I got a geology degree, went on to study the subject for a master's degree and got a job as a geoscientist.'

A levels and alternatives

While, for most students at school in the UK, A levels are the normal route into higher education, this is not an exclusive pathway. Other routes include taking BTEC National qualifications, the International Baccalaureate or, especially for Higher National Diploma courses, NVQ level 3.

There are Access courses for people who were disadvantaged in some way at school, and at that time were unable to achieve the required entry qualifications, and have subsequently decided they want to get back into science at higher education level. There are also foundation courses for those who simply did the wrong A levels for a science degree course, or who are returning to study after a break, or who need to improve their language skills before embarking on a science degree course. Both Access and foundation courses usually take one year, full-time.

Advanced Apprenticeships have also been introduced, e.g. in engineering. These combine learning in the workplace with study and can lead to an NVQ level 3 qualification and thence to higher education.

More and more qualifications are being introduced into the UCAS tariff; for instance, points may be awarded for key skills.

Some recent degree course developments

- An increasing number of modular courses are available which allow you to build up your own degree with a series of short discrete modules covering subjects of your choice.

- A wider range of subject combinations is available, such as languages with sciences or business studies with sciences.

- More new and unusual topics are on offer, such as bioinformatics, medical cybernetics, environmental chemistry, herbal medicine, toxicology, and mechatronics, to name just a few.

- Many courses now include generic or key skills to improve graduate employability, and work experience through links between universities and industry.

- Foundation degrees are employment-related and offer flexible study methods. 60% of the students completing a foundation degree progress to complete a full honours degree. Others study for a professional qualification.

Different types of course

All too many students drop out of higher education because of a change of heart or because the course they chose did not meet their expectations, so do not rush into any decisions. Once you have decided which subject or subjects you are interested in studying (see later in this chapter), you will be faced with another set of choices.

There are many different ways of studying at higher-education level. These are a few of the many questions you need to ask yourself. It's your future. Only you can make the right choice!

■ What *level* and *approach* of course is appropriate for you? There are degrees, foundation degrees, Diplomas of Higher Education (DipHEs) and Higher National Diplomas (HNDs). Diplomas may take a different approach from degrees – e.g. they may include more project-based work. Foundation degrees are employment-related.

■ Are you interested in a *full-time, part-time* or *distance learning* course? Most full-time honours degrees are three years long (four in Scotland). Full-time foundation degrees, HNDs and DipHEs usually take two years. Foundation degrees are designed to be flexible and may be offered over a longer period on a part-time basis, as can some other HE courses.

■ Would you rather study a *single subject* or *two or more subjects*?

■ Would you like to spend time getting *work experience* as part of your studies? *Sandwich degrees* usually take a year longer than other degrees and all include working with an employer. The most common ones offer a year working with an employer after the second year of study. These are known as '211' sandwich courses. Some work on the basis of alternate six-month periods in university and at an employer. These are called 'thin' sandwich courses. In a third model, known as 'thick' sandwich courses, students spend a year with an employer before going to university and another year once their academic studies have been completed. Jane Antrobus (see page 134) took a sandwich degree and did a year's placement in Australia.

■ Would you like to *study in another country* as part of your course?

■ Are you considering *progression from one level of course to another*? There are some extended science and engineering courses where students take an initial foundation year and then progress to the full degree/HND. It is often possible to move from an HND to an honours degree course in a similar subject after completing the HND studies (as Sally Sunderland did – see page 60), especially if that course is at the same college or university. If you have passed a foundation degree, it is also possible to achieve a full honours degree with just 15 months of extra study.

- Do you have some doubts as to your suitability for a particular subject, particularly if you haven't studied it before? Some higher educational institutions make it easier than others for you to *change course*. Sarah Polack (see page 168) found that her biological sciences degree was: '…well suited to me as it is geared at students who wish to study biology, but are not yet certain which particular area they wish to specialise in'. Andy Malone (see page 182) began with a degree where the initial emphasis was on physics and ended with a degree in geology. Not all degree courses are that flexible, however. Most degree courses require you to study other related subjects at least for the first year.

Joint or combined degrees

Joint or combined first degrees can be made up of complementary science subjects such as biochemistry and food science, or contrasting subjects such as science and business studies, or science and languages. These contrasting combinations can often be useful for very specific careers where both subjects will be needed, such as production engineering and management or technical marketing. Broad first degrees can be topped up with a specialist taught higher degree, although this takes a further year or more and financial support may be a problem.

Joint or combined studies graduates often have a wide range of career options. They follow similar paths to graduates with single honours, although more go directly into work and fewer go on to further study. The newer universities and colleges of higher education tend to offer a wider range of combined and modular science courses than the older, more traditional universities.

Enhanced degrees

Some single subject honours degrees are enhanced by the addition of an extra year. These go by the title MSci, MPhys, MChem etc. Courses in this category offer much more opportunity for research projects and are an excellent precursor to postgraduate scientific research.

Four-year degrees have a number of important advantages. First, they are much more acceptable in other European countries than the three-year BSc because degrees in mainland Europe are longer than in the UK. Second, they give students a much deeper appreciation of their subject than shorter courses. Third, they lead more easily to chartered scientist status than do BScs. Most of the professional bodies offer the chance to become a chartered scientist – for instance, David Long (page 97) is a chartered physicist, a chartered scientist and on the way to becoming a chartered engineer. Four years of study is one of the requirements for chartered status. It is recognised in some consultancy situations, especially in international projects. However, enhanced degrees are not necessary if you decide to teach or pursue a career outside science. While many scientists pursuing a research or an academic career take enhanced degrees, relatively few of them become chartered scientists. This may change as more scientists become chartered.

What to study

One big advantage of taking science subjects at advanced level (e.g. A levels, Highers, BTEC National qualifications) is that you will have a huge range of courses in higher education to choose from. The downside is that this choice can be quite bewildering.

The first questions to ask yourself

- Do I want to build on the subjects I am doing at present and look at courses where these sciences are requirements for entry?

- Shall I look at courses where some scientific knowledge and interest is required, but which take people with a wide range of backgrounds?

- Should I consider courses which will accept students with any advanced-level subjects, even those who have not studied sciences since GCSE?

The important thing here is to remember the one-way escalator idea introduced in Chapter one: it is much easier to become less scientific than more scientific. It is much easier to become less mathematical than more mathematical. If you have A levels in non-science subjects and would like to switch to science, it is not too late (see *What about changing track?* later in this chapter). There are extended science degree and diploma courses that will accept applicants with any A level subjects, by incorporating a foundation year at the start of the course, covering the science and maths subject knowledge you will need. However, if you choose to go for a degree in a subject such as law or business studies it is difficult to get back into sciences later on.

At some stage you will have to decide how broad or narrow you wish your course to be. Do you want to concentrate on one specialist area and build up more in-depth knowledge? This may be with a view to taking your interest further in a job, in research and development or in studying for a higher degree. You may, on the other hand, want a wider course which covers all aspects of, say, chemistry right up to finals, or which includes at least two basic science subjects throughout. You might choose a course like materials science or environmental sciences which call on a variety of basic sciences in a multidisciplinary approach to a major topic. There are also some very specialist degree courses in subjects like minerals surveying, textile chemistry, avionic systems, or prosthetics and orthotics, which lead towards very specific job areas.

What do you want to do after you graduate?

When you are making a choice of what to study, it is wise to look ahead and investigate the career options that will be open to you at the end of a course. Although some people begin higher education with a definite career plan, they are in the minority. Most develop their skills, discover more about themselves and change their ideas as their studies progress. Lots change their minds about their original choice of course and about their career aims. Many are still undecided about their career direction even when they graduate.

Fortunately, most university and college courses are flexible enough to allow for change and development. But it does vary, so bear this in mind as a factor to look for when choosing a course. Such flexibility will help to keep your options open and give you the chance to experience some new areas before you are fully committed. When you consider possible courses, find out at what point you have to make your final decision on your degree subject, or subjects.

More or less technical: it's up to you

The direction you take will depend largely on your own interests and how they develop. If you are considering scientific research, either in industry or as part of a higher degree, it would be wise to choose a fairly conventional single honours degree programme. If you are sure you want your science degree to be part of a general scientific education – a base on which you can build either job training or further qualifications – you will not be disadvantaged by taking a broader first degree. In fact, in an area where you can use sciences in a particular work setting, such as information management, patent work or scientific journalism, it could be a real asset.

If you want to use your science degree in a completely unrelated field, such as in finance, it will not matter very much which way you go, although it is always an advantage to have done well, even if you don't want to continue with the academic subject. Employers are more impressed by someone with a good degree who wishes to change track, than by people who look as if they are abandoning their subject because they were not successful. Getting onto a postgraduate course (and obtaining funding for it) is also a lot easier if you have a good degree – i.e. usually an upper second class or a first class honours.

Bear in mind that there are dangers in too narrow a specialisation. Your interests could take you into a very specific area where there may not be many jobs. On the other hand, you could suddenly become the most sought-after specialist on an unforeseen problem or development. You might strike it lucky, with employers falling over themselves to entice you to work for them. These situations are not easy to predict, but they do happen.

Whole areas of science, such as genetics, biotechnology and nanotechnology have emerged and developed when breakthroughs were made in basic research. People worked on these areas long before they became part of the science courses in universities, so there is a constant reassessment of scientific knowledge and a demand for skills that is very hard to predict. Who knows what kinds of skill will be in demand in four or five years' time? What is certain is that employers will always be attracted by numerate graduates who can analyse and solve problems, work in teams and communicate effectively. Studying for a science degree gives you the opportunity to develop all of these skills.

Maintain your mathematics base

Because mathematics is such an essential tool for sciences it is important to try to take it as far as you can, even if you are not considering maths at advanced level. So persevere at GCSE and try to take the higher tier papers rather than intermediate. That way you won't miss out on important concepts which will be useful if you decide to do science A levels, or equivalent. If you are not sure whether you are capable of taking a full maths A level, remember that passing the first year of the course will give you an AS qualification. Discuss the options with your teachers. Remember that the further you progress in mathematics, the more it becomes a language of ideas and less a matter of doing calculations.

Mathematics at A level currently offers several different syllabuses. You should discuss with your teachers what is available in your school and which option would be most useful for your A level combinations and future career.

If you are taking a science-based vocationally related qualification (such as a BTEC or an A level in an applied subject), you should try to enhance it with as much extra mathematics as you can cope with.

Courses that require sciences at advanced level

First, there are courses in subjects you are very familiar with from school – the basic sciences:

- mathematics
- physics
- chemistry
- biology.

Then there are science subjects you might have come across at school or college. These rarely require an advanced-level qualification in that particular subject for acceptance onto a degree course, although A levels or equivalent in other sciences may be required.

These include:

- geology (or earth sciences)
- environmental science
- computer science
- psychology.

In addition, there are courses offering combinations of these subjects and different ones.

The minimum entry requirement for a degree course is normally two A level passes (or equivalent), plus five GCSEs at grades A*-C (or equivalent). A vocationally related qualification may have to be supported by an academic qualification, e.g. an AS or A level. Adults with relevant knowledge and experience may be accepted with fewer qualifications, or after an Access course. The entry requirements for diploma courses are more flexible, but are likely to be of the standard of one A level. There are no nationally set entry requirements for entry to a foundation degree – work experience may be taken into consideration.

Deciding on a subject/s

The following part of the chapter is intended to help you find a higher education subject (or more than one subject) that interests you. Various angles are used to help you think about the options.

Subject ideas

Subject titles do not always give a clear idea of what the courses are about. Make a list of the ones that interest you and find out more about them by reading the university prospectus in detail. If there is a professional body which seems to relate directly to the content of the course, check whether they approve of it. Beware of courses that look similar but are not. One, such as dietetics, may lead to a professional qualification while another, such as nutrition, may not. Do not assume that a degree course automatically leads to a career in a certain area. More graduates in chemistry, for example, get into forensic science than those with forensic science degrees.

The glossary on page 219 describes some of the scientific subjects offered in higher education. It will help you to choose. You should also refer to prospectuses, UCAS *University and College Entrance: The Official Guide*, also *Which Degree?* and the CRAC *Degree Course Guides* for each subject. You'll find other useful books in the book list on page 207. Also investigate the websites of relevant professional bodies. The Institute of Physics, for example, offers bursaries to some successful students beginning physics degree courses.

On the next few pages there are lists of subjects to give you an overview of the range of disciplines available to you. They have been categorised as follows:

- specialist science subjects, most of which you may have touched on at school

- the main engineering subjects

- specialist engineering subjects

- specialist technology subjects

- medically related courses (which may also lead to professional qualifications)

- courses relating to agriculture

- courses for which some science knowledge is useful, although they are usually open to students with other entry qualifications.

Please note that these lists are only intended to give you ideas – they are by no means fully comprehensive, although they do cover most subject areas. New subject combinations and new courses with new titles are appearing every year. You must get the most up-to-date information before you make your choice. Many of these subjects are available as HND, DipHE and foundation degrees as well as traditional degree courses.

Specialist science subjects – touched on at school

- acoustics
- anatomy
- astronomy
- biochemistry
- biotechnology
- botany
- computer science
- cybernetics
- ecology
- environmental science
- food science
- genetics
- geochemistry
- geography (if a BSc) – some study geography as a social science leading to an arts degree
- geology
- geophysics
- marine biology
- materials science

■ metallurgy

■ microbiology

■ molecular biology

■ nutrition

■ pathology

■ pharmacology

■ physiology

■ plant science

■ statistics

■ zoology

These subjects can often be taken in combination with a basic science subject or with each other. They can even be studied with a completely different subject, such as computing, a foreign language or business studies.

Then there are all the engineering and technology subjects which will normally require maths and physics at A level, or equivalent (except chemical engineering, which requires chemistry).

The main engineering subjects

■ aeronautical engineering

■ chemical engineering

■ civil engineering

■ electrical engineering*

■ electronic engineering *

■ mechanical engineering

■ production engineering

* Many courses cover both electrical and electronic engineering

The engineering institutions, including the Institution of Civil Engineers, the Institution of Electrical Engineers and the Institution of Mechanical Engineers accredit certain degree courses as being an acceptable route to their professional qualifications. If your aim is to become a professional engineer it is advisable to check your shortlist of courses against the list of approved courses given on their websites.

Specialist engineering subjects

- acoustical engineering
- aerospace engineering
- agricultural engineering
- architectural engineering
- automotive engineering
- avionics
- biomedical engineering
- broadcast engineering
- building services engineering
- communications engineering
- computer engineering
- control systems engineering
- design engineering
- digital systems engineering
- environmental engineering
- industrial engineering
- marine engineering
- materials engineering
- mechatronics
- minerals engineering

- naval architecture

- offshore engineering

- plant and process engineering

- software engineering

- structural engineering

- systems engineering

- telecommunications

- yacht and powercraft design

For this group of specialist courses you really do have to find out if the course is what you think it will be and make sure you investigate the employment prospects thoroughly. This is particularly important because specialist courses like these are usually aimed at employment in a very specific industry, and are less likely to be as acceptable in a wide range of engineering jobs as those in the 'main engineering subjects' list. Degree studies on that list often cover many of the specialist topics on this one, so if you are studying for a degree in electronic engineering it would probably cover control systems, digital systems and telecommunications. It is therefore important to read prospectuses carefully. You can also enter a career in engineering with a degree in another relevant discipline. Paul Pilkington (page 120), working in aeronautical engineering, says that his physics degree course:

'... covered all the major topics of the engineering degrees, but in less detail, but also covered subjects like astrophysics, cosmology and particle physics'.

David Long (page 97) also became an engineer after a physics degree.

Specialist technology subjects

- aeronautical design technology

- architectural technology

- audio technology

- brewing

- building technology

- ceramics science

- food technology

- glass science

- internet technology

- leather technology

- materials technology

- medical electronics

- multimedia technology

- television technology

- textile technology

Again, these choices are very specialised and would not be a good choice for someone keen to keep a wide range of options open. Take care to check the employment opportunities before embarking on courses like these.

If you are taking a vocationally related course (e.g. a BTEC or an A level in an applied subject), it is important to check that the mathematical content will be sufficient for entry to the higher education course you have in mind.

Medically related courses

- audiology

- biomedical science

- chiropractic

- complementary medicine

- dentistry

- dietetics

- environmental health

- herbal medicine

- homoeopathy

- medicine

- midwifery

- nursing

- occupational therapy

- optometry

- orthoptics

- osteopathy

- paramedical science

- pharmacy

- physiotherapy

- podiatry

- prosthetics and orthotics

- radiography

- speech science

- sports therapy

- veterinary science

A few of these courses may accept applicants with non-science A levels, or equivalent. Courses in both medicine and veterinary science include many of the subjects listed on page 91, such as anatomy, physiology, biochemistry, pharmacology and pathology, in addition to clinical studies.

Although medical degree courses have expanded in recent years, competition for places is still fierce. Many universities now ask applicants to complete a test in addition to getting good A level grades. There is a Biomedical Admissions test, and a Medical Schools admissions test. Some students start a degree in medicine after they have completed a science degree. Medical schools ask these students to pass the Graduate Medical Schools Admission test.

Courses relating to agriculture

- agricultural economics
- agriculture
- animal science
- aquaculture
- arboriculture
- crop science
- equine science
- estate management
- forestry
- horticulture
- pig and poultry production
- rural resource management
- soil science

Courses for which some science knowledge is useful

- anthropology
- archaeology
- architecture
- catering management
- cognitive science
- computer studies

- geographical information systems

- health studies

- history of science

- home economics

- information management

- landscape architecture

- linguistics

- mapping science

- photography

- psychology

- sports studies

- surveying

- town and country planning

What's your favourite subject?

If these lists seem difficult to use, why not try another way of considering the subjects that might interest you in higher education? Start with your favourite basic science subject at advanced level and see what the option list looks like.

Many of the maths-based courses will also require physics – and vice versa; many of the courses requiring chemistry will also require another science, and those requiring biology may well also need chemistry. Check carefully for exact entry requirements.

Favourite subject mathematics?

The following are just some courses that might appeal to you:

- actuarial science

- aeronautical engineering

- agricultural engineering
- artificial intelligence
- bioinformatics
- chemical engineering
- civil engineering
- computer-aided design
- computer science
- computer systems engineering
- cybernetics
- electrical engineering
- electronic engineering
- geology
- management science
- materials science
- mathematics/informatics
- mechanical engineering
- metallurgy
- meteorology
- naval architecture
- operational research
- physics
- quantity surveying
- software engineering
- space science
- statistics

- structural engineering
- telecommunications.

Favourite subject physics?

The following are just some courses that might appeal to you:

- acoustical engineering
- aeronautical engineering
- astrophysics
- biomedical engineering
- chemical engineering
- civil engineering
- communications engineering
- computer sience
- computer systems engineering
- cosmology
- cybernetics
- design engineering
- earth sciences
- electrical engineering
- electronic engineering
- environmental engineering/science
- geophysics
- materials science
- mathematics
- mechanical engineering

- medical engineering
- metallurgy
- meteorology
- naval architecture
- optometry
- particle physics
- physics
- radiography
- space science
- telecommunications.

Favourite subject chemistry?

The following are just some courses that might appeal to you:

- biochemistry
- biology
- biomedical science
- biotechnology
- catalysis
- chemical engineering
- chemistry
- dentistry
- dietetics
- ecology
- environmental health
- food science

- forensic science

- geochemistry

- immunology

- materials science

- medical biochemistry

- medicine

- metallurgy

- microbiology

- molecular biology

- nutrition

- pathology

- pharmacology

- pharmacy

- physiology

- plant science

- polymer science

- textile science.

Favourite subject biology?

The following are just some courses that might appeal to you:

- anatomy

- arboriculture

- biochemistry

- biology

- biomedical science

- biotechnology
- botany
- dentistry
- ecology
- environmental health
- food science
- forestry
- genetics
- health sciences
- horticulture
- marine biology
- medicine
- microbiology
- nursing
- nutrition
- orthoptics
- paramedical science
- pathology
- pharmacology
- physiology
- physiotherapy
- plant science
- sports science
- toxicology
- veterinary science

- virology

- zoology.

Take the four basic science subjects...

Yet another way of choosing your subjects is to consider the four basic science subjects:

- mathematics

- physics

- chemistry

- biology.

To keep open the widest choice of science and other courses in higher education it would be best to take all four after GCSE! Four full A levels (or equivalent), however, are definitely too much for most people. Taking some subjects to the full A level and some at AS is an option, but this will not give the subjects equal weight.

Deciding which to carry on to advanced level at the end of year 12 needs a lot of careful thought; you need to find out whether you can start three sciences and maths at AS and then continue with two or three to A level at your school or college. You can also take a BTEC National or A level in applied science for a more vocational slant and still be able to apply for a degree course – especially if you also take a mathematics or a single science A level. Post-16 qualifications are supposed to encourage a broader range of subjects, so this might not be seen as a good use of the system.

If you are in Scotland, Highers in year 5 will give you a broad base. In theory, in England, Wales and Northern Ireland, you can do up to five subjects in year 12; in practice, some schools may not be able to offer more than four subjects because of timetabling restrictions. It may also be possible to pick up AS levels in year 13. One of the advantages of the advanced-level qualifications is that you can mix and match subjects and academic or vocational courses. However, your actual choices will depend on what is on offer at your local schools and colleges of further education. Sometimes the school timetable can inhibit the opportunity to study certain courses at the same time. If your school does not offer the courses you want, investigate other schools and colleges. When they say 'you can't do that!' they often mean 'You can't do that here'.

You could take a BTEC National course in sciences

Although this leaves open a wide range of sciences, you might need to do extra mathematics to reach A level equivalence in that subject. A BTEC National leads naturally on to a Higher National Diploma, and is also acceptable for many degree courses – although some still prefer traditional science A levels.

What if I don't have …?

If keeping all your science options open seems too difficult, it may be more sensible to examine your interests in the basic sciences the other way round and look at the consequences of not taking each one at advanced level. Here are some guidelines.

No mathematics?

This would eliminate most courses and careers in maths, physics, engineering and technology. Maths is also useful to support the other sciences at advanced level and in higher education, and would be helpful for other degree courses such as economics and management sciences. If you are quite sure you don't want to go into the more mathematical areas and feel that your interests lie more on the biological and biochemical side, then continuing with maths might not be so important. On the other hand, you might need mathematics in the future and you would be wise to study it for as long as you can. AS mathematics could be worth considering. It is easier to pick up both statistics and biology on your own than it is to make up lost ground in maths if you find you need it later on.

No physics?

This would limit your choice of courses and careers in physics, engineering and technology and in mathematical subjects. There are other careers such as optometry, acoustics and meteorology where physics is involved. If you want to do biological or chemical subjects then physics may not be so badly missed, particularly if you have an appropriate level of mathematics. However, physics does support chemistry and would help you with the molecular aspects of biology.

No chemistry?

If this leaves you with both maths and physics, you still have a range of mathematical, physics, engineering and technology careers to choose from. Some students take maths and physics, perhaps with an arts or social science subject, such as economics. However, without chemistry, you would be disadvantaged in fields such as chemical engineering and other biological and biochemical subjects where chemistry can be as important as biology for some courses. An A level in chemistry is essential if you are interested in medicine, veterinary science or pharmacy.

No biology?

Whilst biology is a popular scientific A level, it is usually regarded as the least 'hard' of the sciences. Quite what this means is rather unclear. Possibly it is because biology is a more descriptive science and many people find the concepts easier to grasp than those in physics.

However, this is changing as the study of biology becomes less about whole organisms and more about what goes on at the molecular and cellular levels. Although in the past, biology was rarely a requirement for entry to degree courses, it is now often requested – e.g. many medical schools are now stipulating biology as a preferred second science subject, either at AS or A level. Biology also counts as a science subject if the entry requirement is for two unspecified science subjects.

Remember that there are opportunities to catch up by taking a foundation or extra year on those degree courses which accept applicants without the necessary science A levels.

What about two basic sciences at advanced level?

The sections above have looked at ways of including as many sciences as possible as well as maths in your advanced-level choice in order to keep open the widest range of options. But many students take only two or even one of these subjects in their advanced-level combinations. This is often because they want to study a wider range of subjects, such as sciences and humanities, or sciences with social science subjects. You might also decide to take a different science subject, such as environmental science or computer science, because it interests you and you feel it would complement your other subjects.

Taking just two basic sciences will clearly narrow your choice at the next stage, but this will not matter if the careers and further courses being eliminated are not ones that you are likely to be interested in. For example, a combination of maths, physics and economics leaves open a wide range of maths, physics and engineering options, but cuts out courses requiring A level chemistry (such as medicine and biochemistry). A choice of chemistry, biology and French would make it difficult to get into engineering and physics-related careers and also those requiring a high level of mathematics.

Again, the best way of reviewing the career options leading from any particular choice of two basic sciences is to look at the careers and further courses being eliminated, or made less easy to enter, by the combination you are considering. You can use the lists above to help you.

Is it worth taking one basic science?

It is not usually a good idea to take either physics or chemistry on its own, unless you are just interested in widening your general education rather than studying sciences beyond advanced level. The most usual single subjects are mathematics (which is useful for economics and business courses) and biology (which is a good foundation for paramedical studies or for those who might find it useful later on, in primary teaching, for example).

A single science A level (or equivalent) is really too narrow a base for most science degrees. However, now that many science courses in higher education (apart from ever-popular courses, such as medicine and veterinary science) are keen to get more applicants, they are becoming more flexible about entry requirements. Supporting AS levels will count towards your entry requirements, and maths and science GCSEs at grades A*-C (or equivalent) may also widen your choices.

What grades will you need?

Choosing subjects on the basis of grades required rather than following your scientific and career interests is not likely to end in success. However, it is also sensible to be realistic: there are some courses, such as medicine and veterinary sciences, where the competition is such that high grades are needed to get in.

Very often the grades required for a degree course depend more on the popularity of the course rather than on the difficulty of the subject. So there are huge variations between universities and colleges in terms of the grades they require for the same subject, as well as for different subjects. There are exceptions: although mathematics and physics, for example, have never had a very high ratio of applicants to places – these courses do attract students with high grades. This is possibly because students feel these subjects would be difficult, or because they have been advised against doing them. In contrast, business studies is an example of a subject which attracts high numbers of applicants who, on average, do not have very high grades. A few of the people in our profiles did not get good enough grades for their first choice of course, but ended up on courses which they thoroughly enjoyed and which have been the basis for successful careers. Bob Simpson (page 117) initially wanted to be a vet.

David Long

Career profile

Job title: reactor control engineer

Employer: British Energy

A levels: maths (pure & applied), physics, chemistry

Degree: physics with space science & technology

University: Leicester

'Mathematics always came relatively easily to me but I found science and its application far more interesting. This led to my opting to study double science and technology for my GCSEs at school.

In my experience, progression to A level resulted in a separation of student scientists into two distinct groups. Most studied maths and many studied chemistry – however, almost all elected to study either biology or physics. Very few people studied both. For me the choice was physics.

As I reached the end of my A levels, I became aware that I was leaning further and further towards physics. I found pure maths a little dry, whilst chemistry was interesting but not captivating. Physics, however, continued to intrigue me with its seemingly mind-expanding theories and obvious applications in technology and innovation. These practical applications indulged my increasing interest in useful science and engineering.

Having decided to continue through higher education by studying a physics degree, I was faced with the vast array of course permutations. Leicester University's degree in physics with space science and technology was my choice. The space science was everything that I hoped it would be. I found it absolutely fascinating and its contribution to my degree kept me going through what was, to me, the less exciting theoretical side of pure physics. The practical side of physics was great too, with long afternoons spent 'playing' in the laboratory. Whilst I still enjoyed much of the pure physics, I began to realise that I was probably not destined for a life of perpetual study, research or lecturing, so whenever I had the option I further diversified my degree by undertaking modules such as medical physics and engineering management.

As I approached the end of my degree, I still wasn't sure what I wanted to do and how, or even if, I would use my studies vocationally. The medical physics module and visit to the Leicester Royal Infirmary meant I seriously considered a career in medical physics. I came very close to taking the relative security offered by a career as an actuary, a profession known to be consistent with the logical and analytical nature of physicists. I was even momentarily swayed by the potential big bucks and frenzied lifestyle of a career in the money markets, another preferred choice of the non-practising physicist.

I finally found my calling when I came across an advert for engineers with British Nuclear Fuels Limited. The advert was part of a nationwide recruitment drive for engineers and scientists. The intention was to reduce the age profile within the industry to combat the very real possibility of a total loss of industry expertise as the existing workforce retired with the outgoing first generation of civil nuclear facilities. During the interview process my studies in physics must have served me well and I was successful. Initially, I was employed by the BNFL Magnox Generation Business Group corporate function in a role described as 'career development'. Essentially, this was an excellent training scheme covering all areas of nuclear power plant design and operation. I was amazed at how much of the pure physics I had studied could be applied. Particle and nuclear physics, thermodynamics, electro-magnetic theory, Newtonian mechanics and many other areas were all brought to life. I was based at Sizewell A power station, in Suffolk, where my programmed training concluded in my being appointed as a reactor control engineer. This job involves the hands-on operation of the power station from the main control room, the nerve centre of the entire operation. It's a 24-hour a day, all-year-round operation. To fulfil this role, a person must become a duly authorised person (DAP), as identified in the nuclear site licence. Effectively, this was like a driving licence for the control and supervision of a nuclear reactor and all the auxiliary plant required for safe electricity generation, except it was far longer and immeasurably more demanding in the training and the authorisation.

The work seemed to click for me instantly and I began to progress through the organisation with previously unheard-of speed. I believe that I was for some time the youngest DAP in the country and I only lost this status through promotion. I amassed many more authorizations, such as senior authorised person for electrical and mechanical and nuclear radiations safety rules, high voltage switching authorisations and the status of emergency response access controller. The health physics training and authorisations I obtained were still grounded in the physics that I had studied. However I found that I had now evolved to describing myself as an engineer first and physicist second. As such, I actively pursued professional recognition and found that my education and my work very easily met the requirements. I am currently a chartered physicist (CPhys), chartered scientist (CSci) and member of the Institute of Physics, and I am in the final stages of attaining chartered engineer status.

I progressed through several operational positions at Sizewell A, culminating in my being appointed as an assistant shift charge engineer. This role combined being a technical specialist in nuclear, electrical, mechanical, and control systems engineering with scientific expertise in physics, radiological protection and chemistry, as well as being a safety professional, an operational consultant, a practical faultfinder and a problem rectifier. I was also required to write detailed technical specifications and instructions, manage risk and risk assessment, carry out investigations and write reports. Ours is a very safety-conscious industry, something that is recognised in countless awards and accreditations such as those presented by The Royal Society for the Prevention of Accidents (RoSPA), Det Norsk Veritas (DNV) and the International Organization for

Standardization (ISO). In fact, Sizewell A has recently become the first business in the world to be given the highest possible safety and environmental awards by DNV, having been given Level 10 certification under the International Environmental Rating System (IERS) and the International Safety Rating System (ISRS).

Having mastered the technical side of Sizewell A, I was left with the choice of moving into senior management for the decommissioning of the station or seeking a new technical challenge elsewhere. All my experiences of management up to this point had been very positive, but I had often found myself looking over the fence. Next-door was British Energy's Sizewell B, the most advanced nuclear power station in Britain. I could not resist the challenge and in 2004 I transferred to Sizewell B. The price I had to pay for this transfer was the loss of all the authorisations I had obtained, the relinquishing of all the responsibilities I had amassed and the forfeit of the reputation and respect that I had worked so hard to attain. The reward was the chance to learn and understand the next generation of the science and engineering that combine to give nuclear power, and that was enough for me.

For nuclear power the future is not readily apparent. Unfortunately, Sizewell A is to be shut-down and decommissioned in the very near future, along with the remaining first generation of British nuclear power stations. The Government has acted by forming the Nuclear Decommissioning Authority to take care of these old workhorses – however, as yet there is no commitment to their replacement. For us to maintain our current carbon dioxide production levels from electricity generation, it would require a wind farm covering an area of 275sq miles to replace one old Magnox reactor power station. I truly believe that as soon as the benefits of nuclear power are objectively considered in terms of environmental impact and security of supply, as compared with the other practical options for large-scale electricity generation, there will have to be a revival of the industry. When that time comes, scientists will be in demand to help shape and control the renaissance.

Throughout my career my studies as a scientist have served me very well. I know from personal experience that the skills and knowledge acquired studying science are practical and transferable. Compared to some subjects, the workload may be demanding and the content challenging. However, in a society where every other person is able to achieve a purportedly equal level of education I have found that there remains industry and business recognition of the scientist's efforts and abilities'.

Information about the grades likely to be attached to offers of places on higher education courses is published by UCAS in *University and College Entrance: The Official Guide* (with the accompanying CD ROM), and also in *Degree Course Offers*, published annually by Trotman. Remember, this information may help you to look at your applications realistically but should not be used as the sole basis for your choice.

As higher education absorbs more students, there is now a wider spread of offers. There is a trend towards valuing communication and teamwork skills and other non-academic attributes, as well as exam passes, when offering places. However, the table below shows that point scores have generally increased since 2002.

Many colleges of higher education will accept students with the minimum two A level passes (or the equivalent) onto degree courses. Competition in the long-established universities is generally the keenest, and grades normally play a very significant part in selection, although at present there is a shortage of students with sciences at advanced level.

For applicants accepted by institutions in the UCAS scheme over the past few years, the league table of points is given below. When reading this table remember that these are average point scores and there are many courses, both at old and new universities, that will take students with lower point scores. Others, on the other hand, including Oxford and Cambridge, will require very much higher scores for all subjects.

Average points* required by institutions in the UCAS scheme

	2002	2003	2004
Pre-clinical medicine	433	429	442
Mathematics	385	390	401
Computer science	166	166	170
Physics	374	384	395
Chemistry	307	312	334
Biology	271	278	294
Geology	294	302	303
Pre-clinical veterinary medicine	429	444	438
and for comparison – some non-science subjects:			
Media studies	183	183	195
French studies	300	313	327
History (by period)	318	328	259
English studies	296	307	320

* rounded to the nearest whole number

Source: UCAS

UCAS tariff (including Scottish qualifications)

GCE A level points	AS level points
A = 120	A = 60
B = 100	B = 50
C = 80	C = 40
D = 60	D = 30
E = 40	E = 20

GCE A level (double award) points	
AA = 240	CD = 140
AB = 220	DD = 120
BB = 200	DE = 100
BC = 180	EE = 80
CC = 160	

Scottish Higher points
A = 72
B = 60
C = 48

Scottish Advanced Higher points
A = 120
B = 100
C = 80

The UCAS tariff is a points system for entry to higher education. It replaces the previous system and includes other qualifications, such as vocational A levels and Scottish Highers/Advanced Highers. Some universities still choose to express their entry requirements in terms of grades.

Grades required by BTEC holders

For entry to degree courses, students with BTEC National qualifications are usually expected to achieve several Merits and, for some courses, Distinctions too. Again, details are available in UCAS' *University and College Entrance: The Official Guide* and *Degree Course Offers*, published by Trotman.

A levels in applied subjects

In Autumn 2005, vocational A levels/AVCEs were restructured in line with GCE A levels. A and AS levels in applied subjects are designed to introduce you to a broad vocational area, and most can be taken as double-award qualifications. The A levels in this group include A levels in applied science, applied ICT and engineering. If you are taking such courses, you need to research entry qualifications carefully: if an A level in an applied subject is offered, many science-based degree courses will also require maths A level, or perhaps an A level in a particular science subject. A levels in applied subjects on their own may be acceptable for some vocational degree courses, however.

Combining sciences with other subjects

Many people choose a mixture of advanced-level subjects by studying social sciences, humanities or creative subjects alongside science. This can work well; it can give you a more varied programme and will allow you insights into a range of very different subjects. However, it will cut down the range of higher education and career options ahead, just as when you reduce four sciences to three, only more so. Think carefully, in case you decide to continue with science later on. Taking other subjects at AS level only is one way of broadening your subject base without minimising your options.

In Scotland, where students are able to choose five subjects for Highers, most students wanting to do sciences are encouraged to do at least one social science or humanities subject.

What about changing track?

If you are quite sure you want to leave science behind there are many courses which will take students with any A level or equivalent qualification: accountancy, economics, philosophy, business studies and law to name just a few. For some, but not all of these courses, mathematics at A level or equivalent will be required.

The range of non-science degrees open to people with science A levels is considerable. Certain science courses, like computer sciences, sports science and environmental studies, may accept people with A levels in other subjects. There are also science, engineering and technology courses where students without science A levels or equivalent can complete a foundation course or a preliminary intensive science year before going on to a degree course alongside those with science qualifications. Mathematics at GCSE grade A*-C is usually required. A few medical schools also offer one-year pre-medical courses for students with non-science A levels, or equivalent qualifications. These courses are extremely competitive and usually require very high grades and evidence of strong motivation.

Details on these courses will be in the UCAS' *University and College Entrance: The Official Guide* and other publications in the booklist (page 207).

What help can you get?

■ Use the careers and higher education information and guidance resources listed in the booklist on page 207. They may be available in your school, college or careers/Connexions centre library.

■ Talk to your science teachers.

■ Read more about the courses on offer in prospectuses, higher education handbooks and databases. Widen your general science knowledge through magazines such as *New Scientist*, the science pages of the quality newspapers, 'popular' science books and biographies, TV and radio programmes, visits, lectures, open days and 'taster' courses at universities.

- Visit the websites of the major scientific institutions.

- Talk to your personal/careers adviser.

- Talk to someone who has completed a course that you are interested in, if you can.

- Ask local employers and investigate the websites of large national and international employers who may interest you.

- Try some work experience or holiday jobs.

- Discuss your thoughts with family and friends.

A final word

This chapter is just a starting point. There are many other things to be done before you can reach a decision about what to do in higher education. There are new ideas to consider, people to talk to and other sources of help and information to explore. The lists earlier in this chapter do not cover every option: there are new courses offered every year and all sorts of combinations you will never have heard of that may be available at just one or two institutions.

So you must consult the most up-to-date sources of information about higher education, particularly the UCAS website or reference books such as UCAS' *University and College Entrance: The Official Guide* and the others in the booklist on page 207. Also, study the Glossary of science courses on page 219. It is most important that you find out what the science courses that interest you are about, particularly if you have not studied the subjects at advanced level. Don't just assume that you know: make sure you understand what is involved.

Consider the stage you are at now, and decide where you are in your career planning. Draw up a plan of action using the suggestions in this book and then add your own. For example, you might want to talk to someone who is already in a job that interests you. If you need a professional qualification to get into the career of your choice, check that the courses you are considering are accredited by the relevant professional body. The more you find out, the more your interests will clarify and new ideas will grow. Make sure that you choose the right course, the one which will suit you best, because that is how you will gain success and satisfaction.

Chapter five
Where will your science degree lead?

SCIENCE DEGREE

This chapter covers:

■ the main ways that people use their science degrees

■ graduate employability, the worth of a science degree and what science graduates can offer employers

■ the nature of a graduate job

■ how graduates find work

■ the destinations of science graduates

■ examples of careers entered by science graduates and profiles of scientists who have developed their careers in different ways.

Using your degree

The penultimate year of your degree or diploma course is the best time to take stock and consider the options open to you. Many employers offer summer vacation work, sometime called internships, to those who are about to embark upon the final year of their degree. Taking these opportunities is a good way to test out careers that may interest you, and recruiters often use these experiences as a way of finding new graduate trainees. In any event, it is unwise to complete your studies without gaining some work experience and for many students these days it is a financial necessity.

Most students, however, don't get around to thinking about their future until the final year of their degree and a significant proportion leave it until they have graduated. There are lots of activities you can get involved in during your final university year that can improve your chance of getting the career you want. They include careers fairs and employer presentations at which you can learn more about many employers. There may be skills workshops, aptitude tests, personality questionnaires, careers talks, mock interviews and a whole gamut of events that will help you make your career decisions. You can look again at your chosen science subject, or subjects, and decide whether or not you want to continue your studies in more depth. Now is the time to explore all the different ways you can use your first degree in the next stage of your career. Professional bodies, such as the Institute of Physics, provide lots of useful information on their websites, often including lists of firms that habitually recruit graduates in their discipline. These are well worth exploring. The Geological Society is among those that organise career days for final-year undergraduates at which you can meet graduates from that discipline and discover the kinds of work they have gone into.

Three directions you can take

- Build on your scientific knowledge with further study, or research and development work in a related area.

- Add to your scientific knowledge with a related vocational qualification or by gaining work experience in an area where a science background is required.

■ Use your degree subject and the other skills you have acquired in higher education to train in a completely different field.

Graduate employability

The Government is keen to improve the 'employability' of graduates, and most universities now have an employability policy designed to make everyone aware that, for most students, education is a means by which they improve their ability to get a suitable job. See www. employability.ukhe.com

The main options when you graduate are to get a full or part-time job, take another course, go travelling, take time out for some other reason or become unemployed. Unemployment for females is significantly lower than for males. Across all graduates in 2003 female unemployment was 5.4% and male unemployment 9.2%. Some argue that this is because women graduates are less 'picky' than men about their choice of first job. Some believe that women are generally more organised and proactive than men in their job search. Perhaps they take it more seriously because they believe that they will have more difficulty getting employment than their male colleagues. Others feel that so much is done these days to help women get into science (see Useful addresses – Women, page 215) that the men are being left behind.

Science graduates who want to be scientists are much more likely to go on to a higher degree than graduates in engineering and computer science. This is because the scientific research community and industries employing scientists, such as pharmaceuticals, place much more value on postgraduate qualifications than do the engineering or IT industries. In the latter it is expected that most graduates in relevant disciplines will go straight into work in those sectors. The high unemployment recorded for computer science graduates reflects the situation in the early 2000s when jobs in IT and telecommunications were scarce. In the 1990s unemployment among computer scientists was very low indeed and by 2005 it had come down significantly from 2003 levels.

All universities and colleges offering degree courses have careers services to help students with their career choices and with finding jobs or further courses. It is these services that collect data regarding what students are doing six months after graduation. This information is amalgamated with that from other universities and colleges to produce national data. A digest of this is published every year by the Higher Education Statistics Agency and from this information the useful publication *What do Graduates Do?*, available on the Prospects website (www.prospects.ac.uk), is compiled.

Is it worth doing a degree?

In 2005 student debt after graduating was running at an average of £13,500 for each new graduate and that was with university fees of £1,100 per academic year, not those of £3,000 about to be introduced. You may be wondering if it is worth doing a degree at all. A science course is hard work and a degree is a substantial investment of time and money. You and your family may have to make sacrifices to support your higher education and there is an expectation that this should pay off. While in the past students paid their fees before studying, soon they will not pay any fees until after completing their studies. So while student debt will inevitably increase dramatically, it may be easier to cope with because the time pressure will be less acute.

Many parents – and students – feel that the knowledge gained on a degree course should be of immediate use in a job and that being a graduate will give you instant status and enhanced opportunities. Higher education qualifications do pay off. Statistics show that young graduates earn almost 40% more than those without a degree, and this difference in earnings widens even further in older age groups. A degree is a starting point for many rewarding and satisfying careers, but your ultimate success may well depend as much on your personal qualities as on the certificate you receive at the graduation ceremony.

Although the rise and fall of Britain's economic fortunes affects new graduates as it affects everyone, currently, non-graduates are twice as likely to be unemployed than those with a degree. Graduates from sandwich courses often move even more quickly into first jobs than students from other courses. Their work experience, related to the subject of their course, is highly valued, and they are frequently offered their first jobs by their sandwich placement employer. The vocational approach of foundation degrees and Higher National Diplomas is also appreciated by employers.

However, the class of your degree does make a difference to your chances of being employed six months after graduating. A recent study by Claire Smetherton from Cardiff University discovered that 55% of graduates with first-class degrees had 'arranged career related jobs before leaving university' while only 33% of those with lower-second-class honours degrees had done do. Graduates with a first-class honours degree are considerably less likely to be unemployed (or inactive) than those with a second-class degree, and so on down the scale. A higher proportion of graduates with first-class honours degrees stay on for further study and training, so proportionately fewer look for jobs. Some feel that their 'academic values are at odds with those of employers'.

All the evidence shows a continued commitment on the part of employers to the long-term recruitment of graduates, and a growing realisation of the need for a better-educated workforce if we are to keep up with our industrial competitors at home and abroad.

Stand up and be counted!

One of the biggest changes in the employment market for new graduates is that there are a lot more of them than there used to be. Not only are there many more universities producing graduates, but there are also a large number of colleges of higher education. Altogether these institutions now turn out around 176,000 full-time and 20,000 part-time graduates per year. 100,000 of the graduates are females and 75,000 are men. In addition, there are around 22,000 students a year leaving colleges and universities with Higher National Diplomas and foundation degrees – of these 14,000 are females and 8,000 are men. Since the introduction of foundation degrees their popularity has grown, while numbers of those studying HNDs has declined. And we have still not counted the 20,000 people studying for degrees part-time, including students at Birkbeck College London and the Open University, both of which specialise in part-time degree studies. Apart from those going on to take further full-time courses, most of these people are coming onto the job market at about the same time each year.

Currently, more than 43% of 18- to 30-year-olds in England go into higher education – a huge rise since several decades ago when a university education was the privilege of the few. The Government has set a target that, by 2010, 50% of young people will go on to higher education. The main emphasis is on widening participation. There are also a lot of people starting degrees later in life as 'mature students'. Therefore, graduates don't have the rarity value they had when many of your parents were in their early twenties.

Despite the increase in the number of graduates generally, there has been a drop in the number of people graduating in certain subjects, such as physical sciences, engineering and technology. This gives these scarcer science graduates the advantage that the competition for jobs which require their type of degree has not risen as it has for positions open to graduates of any discipline. In fact, there is a shortage of qualified people.

Whereas approximately a fifth of graduates go on to further study and training, a higher proportion of science graduates do so; more than 30% of 2003 chemistry graduates, for example.

What graduates can offer employers

The science graduate who has more to offer than just scientific knowledge and skills is in a strong position. Employers are also very interested in the transferable skills that young scientists learn during their training. This is emphasised by both employers and careers advisers.

Graduates are usually employed for their future potential rather than for any knowledge or experience they bring to their first jobs. They are expected to be 'self-starters' who can plan and organise their own work. As the working environment becomes ever more complex, with new technology and legal requirements, new industries replacing old ones, changing business practices, more advanced products, wider markets, so jobs become increasingly involved and require well-trained, flexible, educated people to cope with them.

Transferable skills

The transferable skills of science graduates – most of which are similar to the key skills you will have gained at school – include the following:

- organisational skills – demonstrated by coping with a heavy workload of lectures, research, practicals and essay assignments; the ability to work to set deadlines, often several at a time, and the ability to prioritise work

- analytical and problem-solving skills – through both theory and practice, science undergraduates learn to ask pertinent questions, to interpret data critically, deal with a number of variables simultaneously and deduce results

- teamwork and communication skills – developed through giving presentations and writing reports, working in a team in the laboratory and elsewhere, cooperating with colleagues and also working as an individual towards a team goal

- flexibility and adaptability – on science courses with a multidisciplinary approach, students have to take on board a wide range of scientific theories and techniques

- numeracy and computer skills – with statistical knowledge, familiarity with mathematical software packages and experience of detailed data analysis, science graduates make numerate and computer-literate employees.

These, and other skills, can be readily transferred to the workplace and added to your technical know-how. The articulate, numerate and, even better, literate science graduate may have an advantage over non-scientists, even in competition for more generalist jobs. However, science graduates without these skills can be left behind unless they can compensate with really outstanding scientific ability and technical skills. A few very bright scientists work quietly away on their own, but they are a tiny minority. Proficiency in areas like organisation, teamwork and communication becomes essential for all young science graduates, especially when the job market is tight.

What is a graduate job?

There is much discussion about what constitutes a graduate job and what distinguishes it from any other job. There are some professions, such as medicine, pharmacy or veterinary science, where it is essential to have taken the relevant degree in order to do the job. However, there are many other areas of work where the rules are far less clear cut.

Young graduates are attractive to many employers because they do not need as much training and require less supervision than school-leavers (although there are sometimes unfavourable comments in the press about the lack of literacy, numeracy and other transferable or key skills of some graduates!). The jobs themselves have changed too. There are science graduates now taking lab technician jobs in the place of school-leavers who would in the past have trained on the job. This is an inevitable consequence of more people going on to higher education: employers looking for good candidates now take graduates because people who might, in the past, have left school at 18 are now doing degrees.

There are many reasons why graduates might initially take such jobs: few highly competitive opportunities in the area in which they really want to work; accumulated debts from student days; uncertainty about what they want to do, for instance. But many graduates, especially those who have left job seeking until their final degree exams are completed, take jobs which do not require a degree just as a temporary measure, until the right job turns up. Even an 'unsuitable' job can put you in the right place at the right time, if you take every opportunity to prove your potential for better things.

So a graduate job is best defined as any job a graduate is prepared to do. We do hear stories of the graduate milkman, the PhD postman, etc, but remember, these cases are newsworthy because they are not the norm. Someone who has worked for three or more years to pass academic exams can and should expect a rewarding career that reflects their academic achievements.

On graduation, there is an expectation of a new beginning and of great opportunities opening up. But it is a mistake to expect that you will have an automatic right to a 'good job' or a 'meal ticket for life' just because you are a graduate. Getting the right job for you depends not only on the opportunities available, but on all sorts of other factors, such as your personal qualities, the skills you have, where you live, where you want to work, what your career commitment is, what kind of lifestyle you want, your health, luck and many other factors.

Bob Simpson

Bob's experience demonstrates how it can sometimes be possible to develop a passion, in his case for swimming, diving and the natural world, into a career; perhaps in ways that may be considered unusual.

Career profile

Job title: diving instructor

Employer: The Underwater Centre, Fort William

A levels & Scottish Highers: biology, chemistry and physics

Degree: applied marine biology

University: Heriott Watt

'I learned to swim back in Kenya, where I was born, and spent lots of time on the beach in Mombasa, investigating the marine life. At boarding school in Scotland the subjects that attracted me most were the ones with the most inspirational teachers. These were art, geography and chemistry. But when the time came for me to decide which subjects I would study for my Scottish Highers I chose maths, biology, chemistry, physics and English. I always enjoyed science subjects at school. For my sixth year A level studies, biology was a clear winner and I gave up my passion for art and geography in favour of studying both chemistry and maths.

At that stage my career ambition was to become a vet, but that was before I realised how stiff the competition for university places at veterinary school would be. When I was looking through university prospectuses, the applied marine biology degree course at Heriot Watt University caught my eye because it offered the opportunity to do diving in the third year. Having got onto the first year of the course, I immediately joined the university diving club as a beginner. It was great fun and by the time I reached the third year of my degree I had qualified as a diver. I used to jump into a car with a few friends and go off to the shore for a dip.

Heriot Watt has an Institute of Offshore Engineering located in Orkney. As an undergraduate I was lucky enough to spend some time there doing survey work as a consultant for some of their clients and helping with the teaching of undergraduates. Part of this was a project investigating reefs and coral serpulid which I completed for my final-year dissertation. Loch Creran in Scotland is the most significant UK site for these worms, which attach themselves to rock and calcify to form coral reefs.

After university I joined Deep Sea World in North Queensferry, working as a member of the dive team. Scrubbing the tanks and feeding the animals were both a part of my work. Next I moved to the Blue Planet Aquarium in Ellesmere Port, doing much the same. Following these experiences, I moved to Boston USA and spent a year working in the New England Aquarium. By this time I had gained lots of experience.

Having returned to Scotland, I am now working as a diving instructor at the Underwater Centre diving school in Fort William. This includes teaching first aid and acting as a standby diver. We are also converting a sewage farm into an aquarium and hope to make it into a visitor attraction. All my previous experience is very useful in this role.

My hobby is breeding pythons. I have been breeding fish since

I was at university but breeding pythons is a relatively new pastime. Here in Fort William, close to the sea and in view of Ben Nevis, I'm enjoying what I do'.

How do new graduates find jobs?

The traditional graduate route into employment is to job hunt in the final year of the degree course. Many of the large national employers visit universities on the 'milkround'. Recruiters travel the country giving presentations about the work they have to offer and invite applications for places on graduate training schemes. Another recruitment method is careers fairs. These are one of the best places to meet employers because they give you a unique opportunity to compare them one with another.

The graduate training scheme route into employment is only taken by a small proportion of new graduates. Many enter employment by applying for specific jobs advertised in the press or on the internet, or by taking temporary project work on short-term contracts. An increasing number become self-employed. Small and medium-sized businesses are now major recruiters of graduates; it's no longer just the domain of the 'blue chip' companies.

Much job searching and applying is now done online via the internet. Web-based recruitment is a key route to a job these days, with sites such as milkround uk, hobsons, doctor job and prospects all providing details of career opportunities, employers and, most importantly, vacancies. It is possible to send your CV or completed application form instantly, to any employers you are interested in, and also to find out about any vacancies they may have. There has also been a growth in telephone and internet interviewing at the first stage of selection.

Some employers prefer to recruit graduates with one or two years' experience, possibly trained expensively by other employers, rather than recruit graduates fresh from university or college. By selecting more experienced applicants, some employers recruit workers with higher levels of maturity and personal and communication skills, together with the ability to perform effectively from day one.

Experienced recruits tend to remain with an employer for longer too. This means that for many new graduates the first job can be seen as a stepping stone to better prospects a year or two ahead. However, legislation is coming that will outlaw age discrimination. The effects that this will have on graduate recruitment are not yet clear. It should stop employers from discriminating against older students but it may also reduce their preference for young new graduates.

Paul Pilkington

Paul always wanted to be an engineer, so his choice of degree may not seem like the obvious one to make. He found work through a graduate training scheme.

Career profile

Job title: lead engineer

Employer: Airbus

A levels: maths, physics and computing

Degree: BSc physics

University: Reading

'At school I was always fascinated by how things worked, I enjoyed taking things apart and trying to put them back together again. My major interest has been in cars, so a career in engineering was the logical choice. For GCSEs I was pointed towards maths, physics and computing with a foreign language (German) as a good basis for heading down the career path as an engineer. I also took geography, English and craft design (engineering). At A level I was worried about what degree I would need to get into the motor industry. My enquiries gave me the impression that I would need sponsorship from a company and high A level grades to get into the motor industry as a graduate. I was taking maths, physics and computing. This was supposedly the right combination.

In the end I chose to study for a degree in physics instead of engineering. It covered all the major topics of the engineering degrees, but in less detail, but it also covered subjects like astrophysics, cosmology and particle physics. I enjoyed my degree at Reading; it was around 50% theory and 50% practical. From my point of view I was taking things apart to find out how they worked again!

When I graduated I applied for quite a few jobs covering electronics, vacuum systems, aerospace and television and I accepted a position at British Aerospace Airbus (now Airbus) on their graduate training scheme. This gave me four placements in the first year and a single placement in the second year. In the first year I covered project management, test support (building new testing equipment) and fuel systems (for six months). During the second year, my role within the fuel systems department grew and my responsibilities included looking after aircraft in-service issues as well as the design of components for a new model. This established me as a member of the fuel team. On some of the tasks, I was supported by Airbus employees based in France and Germany. In addition, through the company's Education Resource Centre, I took part in a scheme run by the graduate employees themselves, going into schools to show pupils in practical ways how an aircraft is designed and manufactured.

The fuel team has always been a place where being able to adapt is essential. Over the last two years, I have worked in various roles, including on-call support engineer and developing control concepts for a new variant of a current aircraft. The experience has led me to my present role on the Airbus A380 programme. This has included developing the refuel system architecture (fuel flow analysis) and, now, thermal simulation work for the same aircraft. Along with practical engineering experience, I have been working closely with other Airbus systems teams located in Germany, France and Spain, suppliers of systems equipment and structures teams. I have had to develop an understanding of how the plane becomes certified for flight with the airlines.

Currently, I am working on the testing of the A380 aircraft and based in Toulouse. I have had plenty of opportunity to improve my management skills by leading a team through the development and testing of an aircraft towards certification.'

First destinations

When you graduate, you will be looking for a first job: remember you will not be stuck there for the rest of your life. Even if you think you have made the right choice, you will almost certainly change jobs as your career progresses.

Not all graduates look for work immediately after finishing their courses. Many science graduates go on to higher degrees or take training courses for specific jobs, such as teaching and law. Others do not know what they want to do. They may need to take stock of things, do voluntary work, short-term unskilled jobs or spend a few months travelling. Many of these people will be counted as unemployed in the statistics collected each January on those who graduated the previous summer, but 12 months later they could well be on training courses or in permanent jobs. Today there are so many routes from higher education into work that the first destination figures can only give part of the picture.

The following table shows the first destination by category of graduates completing single subject degrees in maths, physics, chemistry, biology, and environmental science in 2003. For comparison, first destinations of those completing degrees in information technology, electrical and electronic engineering and mechanical engineering are included, along with all graduates.

Key

A = in UK employment

B = in overseas employment

C = working and studying

D = studying in the UK for a higher degree

E = studying in the UK for a teaching qualification

F = other further study or training in the UK

G = further study or training overseas

H = not available for employment, study or training

I = believed to be unemployed

J = other

Science graduate destinations 2003 (%)

	Maths %	Physics %	Chemistry %	Biology %	Environmental science %
A	48.0	40.4	46.9	54.8	57.0
B	1.7	1.3	1.9	1.9	2.2
C	11.2	8.0	5.9	5.8	6.3
D	12.2	27.1	25.2	12.0	10.9
E	8.2	2.8	3.9	5.0	4.2
F	3.4	2.5	2.8	4.1	2.6
G	0.3	0.5	0.7	0.1	0.1
H	6.0	5.5	4.2	6.1	7.6
I	7.1	10.0	6.3	8.1	7.1
J	1.9	2.0	2.2	2.1	2.0

	Information technology %	Electrical & electronic engineering %	Mechanical engineering %	All graduates %
A	63.7	61.3	65.3	61.1
B	1.0	1.9	2.2	1.9
C	6.3	6.4	6.9	8.7
D	6.0	8.4	7.3	6.4
E	1.1	0.6	0.7	2.7
F	2.1	2.2	1.4	4.6
G	0.1	0.1	0.2	0.2
H	4.3	4.0	4.9	5.4
I	12.1	12.7	9.0	6.6
J	3.2	2.3	2.0	2.3

Source: 'What Do Graduates Do?' 2005 (see acknowledgements)

Points to note

- The figures in the tables are rounded up or down, so may not add up to 100%.

- Medical and veterinary graduates are excluded from the tables, as more than 95% of them go on to clinical training.

- HND holders are not included, but see table below.

- Physics and chemistry graduates are more likely to continue further study than other graduates.

- Fewer engineering graduates than science graduates take higher degrees; they need relevant work experience after an accredited first degree to gain a professional qualification.

- Students who are on sandwich courses in science and technology are among the quickest to find jobs, often with an employer they have worked for as part of their industrial placement.

Foundation degrees and HNDs

Nearly half of those who complete their studies for foundation degrees or HNDs go on to study for a degree. Unemployment is much lower among this group, probably because they develop closer relationships with employers during their studies than many graduates do.

	%
In UK employment	28.2
In overseas employment	0.5
Working and studying	16.6
Studying for a degree in UK	43.5
Undertaking further study and training in UK	2.7
Not available for employment, study or training	2.0
Believed unemployed six months after completing studies	3.9

Source: What do Graduates Do? 2005 (see acknowledgements)

How are science graduates employed?

Over half of all vacancies for graduates are for people from any discipline – humanities, science, social science, etc. With a science degree, you could apply for the wide range of jobs which require a scientific background or apply for one of these. It is the flexibility of a science degree that can offer science graduates an advantage over other graduates in the hunt for their first job. Science graduates can potentially be recruited to every activity within a large company. If science graduates have the additional skills and the motivation to secure these openings, they will clearly have an advantage.

To give you an idea of how science graduates are employed, below are just some examples of the kinds of careers they can enter. A specialist degree, further training or postgraduate qualifications may be needed for many of the jobs listed. It is by no means an exhaustive list.

Graduates from biology courses

You could consider becoming a:

- laboratory technician
- biology teacher
- marine biologist
- clinical research associate
- audiologist
- research molecular biologist
- immunologist
- biomedical scientist
- microbiologist
- environmental health officer
- clinical scientist
- food scientist
- forensic scientist
- patent agent
- quality control technician
- conservation officer
- medical salesperson.

Graduates from chemistry courses

You could consider becoming a:

- research chemist
- chemistry teacher
- scenes of crime officer
- analytical chemist
- quality control chemist
- forensic scientist
- industrial chemist
- food technologist
- medical laboratory technician
- pharmacological formulation scientist
- health and safety officer
- technical sales person.

Graduates from computer science/information technology courses

You could consider becoming a:

- web developer
- software engineer
- computer consultant
- IT manager
- systems application specialist
- computer analyst
- IT support officer
- computer programmer

- systems developer

- IT teacher.

Graduates from engineering courses

You could consider becoming a:

- production engineer

- electronic engineer

- civil engineer

- chemical engineer

- design engineer

- engineering consultant

- aeronautical engineer

- development engineer

- mechanical engineer

- electrical engineer

- systems engineer

- structural engineer

- control engineer

- performance engineer

- service engineer

- hardware engineer.

Graduates from environmental science courses

You could consider becoming a:

- conservation worker

- land surveyor

- environmental planner

- rights of way officer
- cartographer
- pollution inspector
- laboratory technician
- environmental consultant
- wastes/recycling manager
- environmental scientist.

Graduates from mathematics courses

You could consider becoming a:

- statistician
- actuary
- computer programmer
- mathematics teacher
- stockbroker
- business analyst
- investment analyst
- auditor
- accountant
- financial manager
- operational researcher
- supply chain analyst.

■ Graduates from physics courses

You could consider becoming a:

- medical physicist

- research scientist

- meteorologist

- systems engineer

- reactor physicist

- audiological scientist

- biomedical engineer

- physics teacher

- statistician

- seismologist

- development scientist.

Points to note about these lists

- In addition to the examples of careers listed here, graduates can enter a career in scientific research, administration (e.g. in the Civil Service), sales, management consulting, the financial services, the Armed Forces, management, journalism, publishing, marketing and computing/information technology.

- Just under half of entrants to careers in computing do not have a degree in computer science or IT.

- The proportion of graduates going into employment related to their subject varies; computer science can claim over half, while only around one in eight biology graduates enter scientific jobs.

Teacher training

In recent years various measures have been introduced to make teaching an attractive option for science graduates. Trainee maths and science teachers on initial teacher training secondary courses in England in shortage subjects receive a bursary of £7000 (£9000 from 2006 when the PGCE course fees will also increase by around £2000). They will also receive a 'golden hello' on starting their second year of teaching – currently, this is £5000 for maths and science teachers.

More information can be found on: www.tda.gov.uk

If you train to teach through a postgraduate certificate of education (PGCE), a substantial proportion of your first degree must be relevant to the National Curriculum. Applications for places on these courses are made through the Graduate Teacher Training Registry. Check requirements carefully. It is also possible to train to teach by working in a school and learning on the job under the Graduate Teacher Programme. Those taking that route are paid a salary as an unqualified teacher – currently £13,500 p.a.

Diana Robertson

Diana Robertson always enjoyed maths at school but, living in Aberdeen – a major centre for the oil industry – she was also interested in geology. In the end she decided against doing what most of her fellow students did – becoming an actuary or accountant – and opted to become a maths teacher. Regrets? She has none.

Career profile

Job title: maths teacher

Employer: Haberdashers' Aske's Boys' School

Scottish Highers: maths, chemistry, physics, geography, French, English

Degree: maths and statistics

University: Aberdeen

'Science was my best subject at school in Aberdeen. It always excited my interest and the practical experiments were fun, especially in the chemistry labs. We had to do English, maths and French for our Scottish Highers, plus three other subjects and for me the clear choice was physics, chemistry and geography. After my Highers I concentrated on maths for my sixth year. I liked the subject and found it easy to perform well in. When I understood and answered a question I knew that it was right and that was a big attraction. In other qualitative subjects you were never so sure. There were no essays to be written, which was a big attraction for me. My English was never as good as my science. But I also loved geography and at university I didn't know whether to do maths or geography. So I enrolled in the science faculty and studied maths, geography, geology and physics in the first year.

I found maths interesting and challenging but also enjoyable. The practical work was hard in physics. At school the experiments had been set up for us by the teachers but at university we had to start from scratch ourselves. I loved geology and, with the oil industry in full swing in Aberdeen, employers were keen on it, but I couldn't see myself doing it as a career.

Many of my friends reading maths at university were going on to careers as an actuary or accountant. I was put off by the long periods of study required to qualify in those professions. So I decided to qualify as a teacher. My plan was that I could then go on to be a teacher or choose to do something else later. I did the postgraduate certificate in education for a year at Aberdeen.

At first I had mixed experiences in my teacher training. Some children were unruly and I found the discipline aspects of it hard. I nearly quit. By the time I qualified I had gained confidence and found that I had a big choice of teaching jobs. I was in demand. I found a great school in George Watson's College. The first year was really hard, but the teaching was very rewarding. I was teaching maths at all levels up to sixth form.

Now I'm teaching at Haberdashers' Aske's Boys' School, a private school in Hertfordshire. I teach further maths and statistics, mostly to A level students, but also to GCSE classes. It's the most popular A level subject at our school. I also organise the 'maths challenge' competition, which gives our children at school more confidence in their ability. My other responsibilities include interviewing prospective students. I also give careers advice to those in year 11, interviewing everyone

one-to-one. Many have had parents who went to university and know quite a lot about choosing a degree course, but a few are the first in their families ever to go into higher education and they need more help.

It's a job I love and I'm still in demand. It's also a flexible job. If I want to I can do maths tutoring at home or work part-time.'

Incidentally, science graduates who particularly want to teach their own single science subject may find more opportunity to do so in the private education sector, as most state schools teach combined science at GCSE level and below. Science teaching is done in a way that integrates physics, chemistry and biology, usually by a team of teachers that together have expertise to cover the entire field.

Career development for science graduates

As we have observed, your first post is unlikely to be a job for life. What happens after this period is much harder to determine. Many people move on to other jobs in two or three years' time. Career development is covered further in Chapter eight, after the chapters on postgraduate study and international opportunities for science graduates.

Science graduates at the top?

The transferable skills of a science graduate as listed on page 115 sound like a recipe for a top job in industry, commerce, government or education, but do science degrees really take people to the top in Britain?

A survey by the Association of Graduate Recruiters indicates that the average starting salary of a new graduate in 2005 was £22,000. Graduates entering work in computing/information technology, engineering and technology were being offered in the region of £21,000 and those choosing to work in actuarial or financial management were being paid £24,000. Trainee investment bankers were receiving £35,000 and those commencing a career in management consulting averaged £28,500.

People in the scientific community are usually more concerned about the low value placed by industry and government on scientific expertise than about salaries alone. This situation is improving, and industry and the public sector do appreciate technical know-how. The shortage of people with scientific, technical and computing skills makes it more of a seller's market for these graduates. However, taking accountancy or management qualifications after graduating can still be a good way for scientists to gain promotion and financial rewards. This option attracts a steady stream of new science graduates and postgraduates.

There is no doubt that starting salaries do affect the choice of a first job, but it is unwise to make the decision on that basis alone. The prospect of three or more years on a very low income may deter you from taking a PhD, but, on the other hand, you might be willing to put up with it for the freedom to work on your own project and your future prospects. There are lots of factors involved in choosing a career: money is just one of them. The career a graduate chooses is often based on how much the job is considered worthwhile, opportunities for training and progression, and sometimes an organisation's environmental record!

One thing is certain: there will be changes ahead. There will be changes both in the way science graduates are used by employers and in what graduates themselves want from their careers. The development of information and communication technology, the increasing globalisation of business, the structure of European and international companies, new scientific developments and the growing recognition of the importance of a strong science base to the future of a successful British economy will all play a part.

Jane Antrobus

Jane chose science because she was interested in the environment. Her sandwich course provided her with an exciting range of experiences, and her career shows how scientific knowledge can be used for the benefit of society.

Career profile

Job title: environmental planner

Employer: Enfusion (an environmental consultancy)

A levels: geography, biology, geology, general studies

Degree: environmental science and geography

University: Bradford

'When I was selecting my advanced-level subjects, I did not have a particular career ambition, but I was advised to take subjects on the basis of enjoyment, hence my selection of geography, biology, geology (and general studies). This has, I believe, provided me with a real interest in my higher education and career thus far.

When I was considering my choice of higher education, my interest in environmental matters and objection to environmental degradation provided me with an aspiration to eventually work in a role where I could play a part in, and exert a positive influence on, environmental management. This, admittedly, rather vague ambition was reflected in the relatively broad subject matter of my degree: a Bachelor of Science in environmental science and geography at the University of Bradford.

My degree included ecology, biogeography, environmental pollution, geographical information systems (computer-based), environmental economics, natural resources, geographical philosophy, statistics and town and country planning.

Before beginning my degree, I had never heard of town and country planning – the control of land use – but I developed a specific interest in the subject as my degree progressed. I chose to carry out my final year research project (dissertation) on this topic. I studied the effect that the physical layout of the neighbourhood of Saltaire (originally developed to house the workers of a large mill) had on the behaviour of its residents (their use of local facilities, the orientation of their social life to the neighbourhood, and their 'sense of place' associations with Saltaire).

My degree was a four-year sandwich course, with the third year taken up by a placement as a voluntary research assistant in the Department of Tropical Environmental Studies and Geography at James Cook University, Australia. Here I assisted with a diverse array of research projects. My placement included:

- monitoring noise generated by tourist aircraft flights on Whitehaven beach in the Whitsunday Islands, a World Heritage Area in Queensland

- assessing compliance by commercial whale-watch operators with regulations regarding the way in which boats approach whales

- assisting with bird, reptile, mammal and amphibian searches in an area of rainforest in East Queensland

- helping to inform the development of a conservation strategy in a desert area in West Queensland by assisting with pitfall trappings, active searches and various other techniques to identify the presence and abundance of species

- conducting face-to-face questionnaires with residents affected by Cyclone Rona – which caused minor structural damage and high flood levels

- studying the response of juvenile reef sharks and stingrays to fake prey items, to determine whether they could detect their prey by their electric signals only.

After graduating, I secured a position as a graduate environmental planner at Nicholas Pearson Associates, an environmental consultancy in Bath. Much of my time was spent assisting with environmental impact assessments. This is a process carried out to determine the likely impacts of a new development on the environment, to reduce adverse impacts and maximise environmental benefits, and to help ensure that developments with unacceptable impacts on the environment are not permitted. My one and a half years in this job provided me with valuable experience working at the interface between development and land use planning, and of consultancy. (Developers, local authorities, government agencies and others employ consultants to carry out work on their behalf.)

I moved on to a position as an environmental planner with Enfusion – another consultancy, specialising in environmental planning and management for sustainability. I have been involved with a variety of projects, including:

■ investigating how much water resources, water quality and flood risk are a constraint on the extensive development proposed for the south-east of England, and what can be done to resolve constraints

■ a sustainability appraisal of a Welsh Development Plan – assessing the likely environmental, social and economic impacts of draft policies, and revising the policies to maximise their contribution to sustainable development for the area

■ an environmental management system for an on-shore oil company, to assess their environmental impacts and improve their environmental performance.

As my career will inevitably evolve, I can't predict where I will be in five or ten years' time. I choose to remain flexible about my future career path, since it will be shaped by my developing interests. However, I would expect to pursue a career based around the subject matter of my current job – people, land use and sustainability. I would also like to return to university to study for a higher degree, which may prompt me to focus on particular specialisms in future. My job would probably not be commonly perceived as 'scientific', but this demonstrates that a science-based education can provide access to a wide range of career paths. The scientific elements of my education have provided me with a sound understanding of the issues with which I work in my current job. If I return to university to study for a higher degree, it will involve the continuation and development of the science and research aspects of my education.'

In conclusion

The dividing line between jobs for scientific specialists and more general positions is not absolutely clear cut: it is possible to move from one to the other. But, as with the choice of advanced-level subjects discussed in Chapter four, the decision made at the end of a degree or diploma course as to whether or not to go further with science is critical. Remember the one-way analogy: it is a lot easier to become less scientific in course and job progression than it is to become more so. It is easier to move from being a specialist scientist to being a generalist than it is the other way round, although Mike Partridge (page 147) is an example of somebody who has gone back into scientific research after starting a career in a more administrative post.

One persistent myth is that a science career is an alternative to a career in management: those who stay in science inevitably become project managers responsible for junior staff, the supervision of laboratories, recruitment and training of their team and budgets. It is probably true that taking the scientific career route provides a smoother transition into management, though some would argue that if you arrive late in management your chances of reaching the top are diminished.

A lot of people with science degrees progress into other jobs either soon after graduating or later on in their careers. In fact, some of the scientists profiled in this book have changed their areas of interest – such as from science into sales or law. Many of the communication and interpersonal skills acquired while doing a science degree are transferable into other areas of work. More and more employers are recognising this, and science graduates now realise that, despite the shortage of scientists and technicians, they must develop these transferable qualities if they are to compete successfully in today's job market.

People are sometimes put off scientific research because of fears that they might find themselves up a career cul-de-sac, but today's specialist skills could be tomorrow's major trend. It would make life a lot easier if we knew precisely which skills will be in demand in the future and where the opportunities will be located, but human resources planning is a very complex activity. While it is possible to make some general predictions, rapid changes in technology and a continuous stream of scientific discoveries make a detailed forecast very difficult indeed.

Chapter six
Postgraduate study – what are the options?

This chapter covers:

- the main options for further academic study and training

- possible funding sources

- some examples of postgraduate courses taken by science graduates.

Why study after a degree?

Each year, nearly 20% of first degree graduates go on to do some kind of postgraduate study or training immediately after their degree course and many more will do so later on, after gaining some working experience. Even though competition for places is fierce, for certain jobs postgraduate qualifications are the only way in, and for others they provide a distinct advantage.

Graduates choose this option:

- for career development
- to develop knowledge and skills in their field
- to gain knowledge of a specialised field
- to change fields
- to improve their career prospects in a difficult job market

■ for scholarship and personal challenge

■ to give themselves more time to decide on their future aims.

Before you make any firm decisions, it is important to ask yourself:

■ Will there be a demand for the kind of postgraduate qualification I am embarking on?

■ Do I still have the motivation and interest to pursue further study?

■ Do I have the funds to continue with further study?

Those with first-class honours degrees and upper seconds are more likely to go on to further academic study because they have a better chance of getting financial support or studentships.

What proportion of graduates go on to further study?

Percentages of graduates going on to further study or training, 2003

	Studying for higher degree (%)	Teacher training (%)	Other training or further study (%)
All graduates	6.4	2.7	4.8
Biology	12.0	5.0	4.2
Chemistry	25.2	3.9	3.5
IT	6.0	1.1	2.2
Maths	12.2	8.2	3.7
Mech. engineering	7.3	0.7	1.6
Physics	27.1	2.8	3.0
Envir. science	10.9	4.2	2.7

Source: What Do Graduates Do? 2005 (see acknowledgements)

Points to note about this table

More science graduates than other graduates, especially physicists and chemists, go on to further study or training at the end of their degree courses. Mathematicians and biologists are much more attracted to a career in teaching than other scientists. The table covers only those going on to full-time further study and not the many others who do part-time further study in their first job or later on. Many employers of scientists encourage them to do higher degrees part-time. Some science graduates decide on their own to return to education full-time.

A wide range of courses

The range of postgraduate courses includes:

- vocational courses, leading to qualifications necessary for particular professions – e.g. PGCE for teaching, Graduate Diploma in Law, etc

- vocational courses which are not compulsory but which would help in particular professions – e.g. engineering geology, petroleum engineering, journalism, human resources, etc

- skills courses such as computer programming, languages, etc

- academic courses leading to certificates, diplomas, master's degrees or doctorates in virtually every subject imaginable.

Qualifications can be gained through:

- research degrees

- taught courses

- part-time study

- modular courses – a 'mix and match' way of achieving postgraduate qualifications through credits or units obtained by open/distance learning – the Open University and other open learning colleges.

There is no state funding support except for postgraduate teacher training (see later), so you will need to find a grant or a studentship or be self-financing. Part-time courses are often done while working, with some financial support from the employer. More details on funding can be found later in the chapter.

There are thousands of postgraduate courses in the UK – some on very specialist topics. So when a course title is mentioned in this chapter it will probably be only one of a number in the same area of work. Only a selected few are mentioned to give a flavour of the range of options available. There are reference websites with comprehensive lists of all the current courses, which you would consult in your final year on a degree or diploma course (see Useful addresses – Postgraduate study).

Higher degrees by research

Higher degrees by research lead to a doctorate (a PhD or DPhil, depending on what it is called by the university awarding it), a master of philosophy (MPhil) or a Master of Science (MSc). Engineers have a special Doctorate in Engineering qualification (EngD) which includes not only research on an industrial project but also management training. A PhD takes a minimum of three years' research, an MPhil two and an MSc one year. The EngD takes four years. If the research is completed on a part-time basis the work takes longer. After a PhD you can use the title Doctor, although you could find yourself having to explain in a medical emergency that you are a scientist, not a 'medical' doctor!

Higher degrees by research are usually taken in a university, research institute or industrial laboratory which has a link with a university. Some universities require all research students to register for an MSc in the first instance and then, if this goes well and finance is available, they continue with their PhD when their progress has been assessed as satisfactory – usually after 12 to 18 months.

For more information about the research degrees on offer, all departments have been given a research rating by the Higher Education Funding Councils, which reflects the quality of the research being carried out, and the publications issued. The top rating is 5*. 2001 results can be found on www.hero.ac.uk. The next assessment of university research will be held in 2008.

Learning to do research

A degree by research involves an in-depth study of a very specific area. Each research student has an academic supervisor who acts as a guide and mentor. The results of the research are presented in a thesis – a detailed written discussion of your project – which must include work that is original and makes a contribution to the understanding of the field.

A higher degree of this type is really a training programme in research, and involves:

- searching through and understanding other written work in the area (called 'the literature')

- constructing hypotheses about a topic

- designing and performing experiments to test hypotheses

- developing and using a range of scientific techniques and equipment

- recording, analysing and interpreting data

- presenting and discussing your findings at seminars and in a final thesis

- cooperating with colleagues both in your laboratory and elsewhere.

Postgraduate research is often seen as a solitary occupation, with students working mainly alone in libraries. This is not true for scientific and technical research, where you are based in a laboratory, interacting on a daily basis with other scientists in your own institute and maybe with scientists in labs around the world, through conferences and computer link-ups. Many researchers are working on real industrial problems and liaise with colleagues in companies. Some have close contacts and collaborations with people in other universities and research institutes, both at home and abroad.

Nonetheless, what counts for your PhD is your own research, both experimenting in the laboratory and the desk work of developing the theoretical basis. Persistence and determination are the two essential qualities of a good researcher, taking pains to learn the necessary techniques and complete exacting, and often repetitive, practical work. Most first degree courses include some project work, in addition to laboratory practical classes, and this experience will give you some idea of whether you would like research work. Although the chosen topic can be important in terms of further career progression, it often turns out that people who make a career of science find themselves working on very different subjects later on.

A higher degree by research is not only a training for academic research; many people with PhD and MSc qualifications also work in industry, teaching, administration and other areas. Employment information shows a very low rate of unemployment among people with PhDs.

Ten years after their doctorates or master's degrees, many senior scientists do very little laboratory-based work. They could be supervising other scientists or may have moved into other areas of work where the training and experience of research is of great benefit.

Funding

Government funding for postgraduate courses is very limited – most coming from the Research Councils – and there is nothing like enough to go around. Decisions are based on various factors, including the class of your degree, your choice of course, and reasons for wanting to do the course. There are other sources of funding, which it would be wise to check out in case your application for a grant is unsuccessful (see Useful addresses – Postgraduate study and funding).

Research Councils

There are six Research Councils (most of them in the scientific field) which offer most of the available funding for postgraduate qualifications. Awards usually cover tuition fees, and a contribution towards maintenance – living costs and expenses – which varies between funding bodies but is in the region of £12,500 p.a. in London (2005/06) and £10,500 p.a. outside London. Engineering doctoral students get £13,500 p.a. Funds are distributed through academic departments, so direct your enquiries through them. Check the extent of the funding. Start your applications in the autumn before your course is due to begin.

Application procedures vary across the UK so check on www.student-support-saas.gov.uk for Scotland and www.delni.gov.uk for Northern Ireland. A list of addresses of Research Councils can be found on page 216. Check each for details of their studentships – the Engineering and Physical Sciences Research Council (EPSRC), for example, offers flexible postgraduate funding through Doctoral Training Accounts and the Master's Training Package.

There are also Co-operative Awards in Science and Engineering (CASE) which support research students working on projects jointly devised and supervised by academic departments and partners in industrial research labs. If the research is sponsored by a company, students also receive additional monies from it, usually up to around £3000 p.a. The Particle Physics and Astronomy Research Council offers an additional year (CASE Plus) where the student works full time on the premises of the firm and receives a salary.

In recent years, the tax-free stipend offered by the Research Councils has increased and in many cases is not much less than an average graduate starting salary after tax has been deducted.

Other forms of funding

One option is to take out a loan. *Career Development Loans* are operated on behalf of the government by certain banks. These are designed to help people study courses that will increase their employability. You can borrow anything between £300 and £8000, to cover up to 80% of your course fees, plus related expenses (100% if you are unemployed). During the course and for a month afterwards the government pays the interest on the loan. For up to 17 months, you can defer the start of your repayments of the loan, if you remain unemployed or are claiming related benefits. Look on www.lifelonglearning.co.uk/cdl or freephone 0800 585505 for an information pack and application form. CDLs are not currently available in Northern Ireland.

Scholarships are offered both by universities and independent bodies such as medical charities and trusts. They are advertised through academic departments, scholarship offices, careers services and the education and specialist press. Investigate the possibility of *European funding*, as this is available particularly in science and engineering.

If you fail to find funding always ask the academics in the university of your choice where previous students obtained their funding from. Also consider taking a paid research assistantship position. *Research and Teaching Assistantships* are advertised in the education and specialist press, e.g. the *Guardian,* the *Times Higher Education Supplement, New Scientist.* Postgraduates are sometimes employed to carry out research. They can also receive direct payment in return for undertaking teaching, laboratory demonstrating and invigilating exams. This is not an easy option as you have to manage a significant quantity of work in addition to your own research. Mike Partridge (next page) funded his PhD studies this way.

A large *trust or charity* may be willing to sponsor an entire scientific PhD project – covering tuition fees, maintenance, laboratory running costs, etc. Others may offer less than £100. *The Grants Register,* published by Palgrave Macmillan, and the *Directory of Grant Making Trusts,* published by Charities Aid Foundation, are excellent sources of major charities.

A research student has to regard this period as an investment in future career prospects. Competition for funding is keen and it is very difficult to get any at all unless you have either a first-class or upper-second degree. The minimum academic requirement for funding of taught masters degrees by research councils is a lower-second-class honours degree but for research degrees an upper-second-class degree is required. Many postgraduates study part-time so that they can hold down a part-time, or even a full-time job to finance their course. Employers sometimes fund employees through postgraduate courses when they feel that there will be a benefit to them from the skills and knowledge obtained or the research that is completed.

Mike Partridge

Mike, who has a PhD in physics, works as a research physicist for the Institute of Cancer Research and the Royal Marsden NHS Trust. He funded his PhD by working as a research assistant and took the unusual step of moving out of research into administration and then back again.

Career profile

Job title: Principal physicist

Employer: The Royal Marsden NHS Foundation Trust

A levels: physics, chemistry, maths, further maths

Degree: natural sciences, Cambridge

PhD: physics, Cranfield

'I left sixth form college with a good selection of science and maths A levels, but no clear idea of the kind of career I wanted to pursue. I chose the natural sciences course at Cambridge University because it allowed me to study a broad range of subjects, only specialising in the final year of the course. I studied the core physics modules but was also able to study chemistry, crystallography, materials science and metallurgy. The skills I learned – combining solid theory with mathematical modelling and careful experimental work – have shaped the way I work ever since.

After Cambridge, I was keen to continue working in physics, but still unsure of where this would lead me. I took a job as a contract researcher with Cranfield University, developing infrared imaging systems and using the work to write a PhD thesis in my spare time. Having completed my PhD, I spent an interesting year working in science administration for the Engineering and Physical Sciences Research Council, which is responsible for allocating research funding in their area of expertise to universities and researchers. This job introduced me to the more political side of research science: working with universities, industry and government to try to decide the best way to target funding for the future. Although I learned a lot working for the Research Council, I decided that what I enjoyed most was being a hands-on research scientist.

My next job took me into the field of medical physics, where I have now worked for ten years. Although my work in this field has been focused completely on improving the diagnosis and treatment of cancer, many of the skills I acquired during my PhD studies were directly applicable. My first medical physics post involved working on very high energy X-ray imaging systems for The Institute of Cancer Research. Medical physics research is a highly complex field, requiring close collaboration between many different professionals: physicists, doctors and radiographers, as well as medical equipment manufacturers. After four years at The Institute of Cancer Research, I left the UK to spend two years working for the German national cancer research institute in Heidelberg. It was a great privilege and definitely a good way to learn to speak German!

Back in the UK again, I got a job as a clinical scientist supporting clinical trials in advanced radiation therapy at the Royal Marsden Hospital. This was a two-year contract and when it was completed I took up my current post within the National Health Service as principal physicist in positron imaging (a very useful diagnostic imaging technique in cancer).

I find academic work in medical physics uniquely stimulating and rewarding. The mixture of clinical work, supervision of students, lecturing and research makes the job varied and demanding. My career path has not been straightforward and has led me into some quite different branches of physics, but with every move have come new challenges and new things to learn; experiences gained in one job always seem to come in useful in the next one (even speaking German!).'

Rachel McCoy

Rachel always enjoyed working in the laboratory and found a personal fascination in science. The research she did for her final year project at university led to a whole range of opportunities, not least a DPhil and her current job.

Career profile

Job title: Senior scientist

Employer: Pfizer

A levels: maths, chemistry, biology, French AS

Degree: Chemistry; DPhil in chemical pharmacology

University: Oxford

'I always enjoyed experiments, even at primary school; the natural world always fascinated me. At secondary school I was lucky to have a very good biology teacher who made the subject easy and interesting. As I progressed I got more excited about organic chemistry and eventually discovered how it coupled with biology.

Even then it was my ambition to be an industrial chemist. I knew that there was a huge deficit of female scientists in industry and decided that I was heading in that direction. I chose maths, chemistry and biology for my A levels. The biology I found really enjoyable and I felt very much at home in the lab. The only downsides for me were when we studied ecology and I had to complete a project on the life cycle of the anchovy. That left me cold. As I progressed I soon found that chemistry was my easiest subject while I viewed maths less positively than the practical sciences. I also studied AS level French, which certainly helped to develop my listening skills. After A levels I chose to study for a chemistry degree at Oxford University. We were able to choose some options during the third year and I chose chemical pharmacology. One of my tasks was to synthesise compounds designed to relax smooth muscle in guinea pigs. For me it brought my two loves of chemistry and biology together. By far the best part of my degree studies was the final year when we got to do a full-time research project. I loved it! And I got to see the project through from start to finish.

My degree completed, I got funding from a pharmaceutical company to profile test compounds in the smooth muscle of the human urethra. It gave me experience of researching in an academic department at Oxford but I was also working on projects of industrial significance. I attended a conference in North Carolina and was employed as a consultant with a research assistant to help me. It began the development of my management skills which would come in useful later.

After 18 months' research I decided to start my studies for a PhD. The project I embarked on was an investigation of the mechanisms involved in smooth muscle control in the lower urinary tract of humans and pigs. It took three and a half years to complete but it was a great joy to be able to work independently and direct my own research. My academic supervisor gave me all the freedom I needed to explore the subject as I chose. I travelled a lot, attending conferences and interacting with industry overseas. I also did some short-term research for a drug company in Chicago.

Luck came my way when I saw an advertisement by Pfizer, the pharmaceutical company, for someone with knowledge of smooth muscle to research it with them. It was right up my street and I'm now working there as a senior scientist in Sandwich, Kent. We have first class laboratories with plenty of equipment. I'm like a kid with a packet of sweets. The research facilities are excellent.

We look at patient needs, study the physiology of disease, and work out what are the most troublesome symptoms and the mechanics of the disease state. I'm employed in the pharmacology discipline group of the biology department but I work with many scientists from different disciplines, all providing their own expertise to tackle the issues. My job includes managing other scientific staff, but I still enjoy working in the laboratory and trying to understand what needs to be done.'

Taught MSc courses

Here are a few examples of taught MSc (master's) course (course requirements are given in brackets):

■ computer software development (degree in any discipline)

■ chemoinformatics (chemistry-related degree)

■ control engineering (graduates of any discipline)

■ human and equine sports science (graduates of any discipline)

■ hydrogeology (science degree plus maths beyond A level)

■ radio frequency communication systems (relevant degree)

■ medical imaging (relevant degree)

■ occupational safety and health (any degree)

■ environmental chemistry (chemistry degree)

■ statistics (variety of different courses requiring different degree backgrounds)

■ operational research (degree with high mathematics content).

The growth in scientific and technical knowledge is too extensive for so many specialist topics to be absorbed into first degree courses, making postgraduate taught courses necessary to cover areas like these. For these courses, a particular subject at first degree level may be required, but this is not always the case. Some MSc courses also prefer people to have appropriate working experience. Master's degrees in areas like information science and clinical psychology involve periods of relevant practical experience and lead to professional qualifications.

A taught MSc usually lasts a complete calendar year full-time or two years part-time. Master's courses include coursework, lectures and seminars, together with practical work and training in research methods. They usually end with a combination of final examinations and a short thesis.

For some science graduates, an MSc is a way of changing career direction. A master's in information technology, actuarial science or marketing can achieve that. For others it is a means of gaining specialist knowledge about an area that may have been broadly touched on by their undergraduate course. A physicist might study acoustics, a chemist may investigate medicinal chemistry and a biologist could take a master's in genetics. Some MSc courses are arranged by employers in collaboration with a university as part of their graduate development programme.

Whatever your reasons for considering further training, you will need to take stock of your situation and do some career planning. Before committing yourself to any master's course read the prospectus in detail and check out the employment prospects carefully. While academics, especially course directors, may give you a rosy picture of the course, the university careers service will have actual statistics about where those who completed the course previously have made their careers. Even though some course titles sound very vocational, there may not be many related job opportunities. Some postgraduate courses recruit a lot of students from overseas, for example, because employment prospects in their own countries will be enhanced. This does not necessarily mean that home students seeking work in the UK will have the same advantage. However, because a full-time MSc lasts only one year, the job situation should not change too much from the start of the course to the end. The experience of recent leavers will help you to predict your chances. Unlike the situation with undergraduate courses, where certain quotas of places must be given to home students, academics are free to allocate most of their places, if they wish, to international students who pay larger fees.

MRes

Another quite different type of course is the MRes. These are skills-based courses on which you learn, though project work and laboratory experience, the skills needed to be a successful scientist. In addition to the practical side of the subject they also include technical writing, presenting and a range of transferable skills. Some students use these courses as a precursor to a PhD.

MBA

One very popular master's course is the Master of Business Administration (MBA). This is taken by many scientists, even those with PhDs, because they want to enhance their opportunities in management. People are strongly advised to gain some working experience before embarking on an MBA course: most science graduates taking an MBA are several years beyond graduation and will have managed other scientists or research teams. There is no government funding for MBAs. The Association of MBAs, which accredits the best courses, offers Business School Loan schemes, via the NatWest Bank and the Bank of Scotland.

Postgraduate Certificate in Education (PGCE)

The best-known postgraduate certificate course is the PGCE. Graduates other than BEds wishing to teach in state nursery, primary or secondary schools require this qualification, which leads to qualified teacher status. The proportion of science graduates taking PGCEs is shown in the table on page 140. Science graduates who apply for a teacher-training course in science need to have taken basic sciences as a significant proportion of their degree course. In order to teach in secondary schools, a large amount of the degree course must have been in National Curriculum subjects. (See profile of Diana Robertson page 130.)

There is a great need for more able and enthusiastic science teachers. At secondary level there is a shortage of science teachers who are science graduates, in particular those with a physics degree. In many primary schools, science graduates have an important role supporting colleagues in the teaching of science and coordinating the science curriculum. Now that science is an important part of the National Curriculum for all ages, primary teachers are required to have studied science to at least GCSE grades A*-C. Even so, only 10% of teachers are qualified in science beyond A level.

A PGCE is the one postgraduate course for which your fees are paid. In England and Wales, aspiring maths and science teachers are paid a bursary of £9000 during training. They also receive an extra £5000 which is paid at the start of the second year of teaching.

Funding for MSc and other taught courses

It is, unfortunately, a lot easier to find an interesting course than it is to obtain funding to do it. As with a PhD application, a good first degree is essential in the competitive funding situation. Some grants are available for MSc courses from the same bodies that support PhD students, although an increasing number of students on full-time MSc courses pay their own way, either with the help of their families or by taking loans.

Part-time students are either self-funded from earnings or supported by their employers. Learning Through Work is an innovative scheme to enable people to achieve postgraduate qualifications through online learning, whilst staying in employment. Students design their own programme of study based on their work and career aspirations to date. Fees are set by the higher education institution. Some of the tuition fee is paid by the Government. Employers may also offer financial support, or help by allowing dedicated time to be spent on study, access to resources, supervision and mentoring.

Courses entered by recent science graduates

The lists below give examples of the range of courses taken by postgraduates.

Graduates in maths

Actuarial science/financial mathematics

Artificial intelligence

Biometry

Education (teacher training)

Housing studies

Hydraulic engineering

Information technology

Meteorology

Numerical solutions

Operational research

Social administration

Statistics

Transport engineering and planning

Graduates in physics

Accountancy

Applied environmental science

Applied optics

Astronomy

Astrophysics

Computer science

Education (teacher training)

Geophysics

Information technology

Law

Materials engineering

Mathematics

Mechatronics

Medical physics

Operational research

Process safety

Radiation and environmental protection

Semi-conductor physics

Teaching English as a Foreign Language

Graduates in chemistry

Acoustics and noise pollution

Administration

Analytical sciences

Computing

Education (teacher training)

Information science

Law

Management studies

Marketing

Material testing

Medicinal chemistry

Organic chemistry

Polymer chemistry

Graduates in biological sciences

Bioinformatics

Biotechnology

Crop protection

Ecotoxicology

Education (teacher training)

Environmental management

Ergonomics

Export management

Forestry

Genetic counselling

Immunology

Information technology

Journalism

Marine resource development

Medical parasitology

Neuroscience

Nutrition

Pest management

Printing and publishing technology

What next after a higher degree?

The careers services in universities and colleges are not only used by undergraduates; if you are on a postgraduate course or are studying for a higher degree you'll need advice too. Most science departments have contacts with industry and with other university departments, both in the UK and overseas. When you decide what you want to do they can help you to make contact with relevant employers, particularly if you are on a specialist course. Most departments should also be able to provide information about the jobs taken up by students who have recently completed their postgraduate courses.

Graduate students doing science PhDs are eligible to attend the UK Grad Programme. The programme provides personal skills development opportunities for postgraduate students through a programme of national residential courses. Courses can be local or national and last for up to five days. For many, attendance is free.

Academic research

If you want to continue in academic research after completing a PhD, you can go on to a postdoctoral fellowship, either in the UK or overseas. These fellowships are seen as a way of broadening your research experience and giving you time to find more permanent employment. British scientists are encouraged to go overseas to do this, and many do – mainly to the USA and continental Europe.

Opportunities to work in a research setting overseas are predominantly in the sciences.

Funding for postdoctoral fellowships, including travel and other expenses, is available from a variety of sources: university departments, Research Councils, charities and European and international organisations.

Research difficulties

Career development for research scientists is always affected by the way research is funded. Recent years have seen many more collaborative projects between science research departments and industry, and more scientists are moving into industry at later stages of their careers.

The trend in research funding in recent times has been towards short-term grants from government and other bodies, with staff in universities working on temporary contracts. Today, in British universities, nearly half of the academic staff in science and engineering departments are on short-term contracts. As a result, the time taken for young researchers to progress to a permanent post has lengthened.

Research science can also put a great strain on young families. Because career advancement and future funding depend on the researcher's early success at postdoctoral level, long and irregular hours in the laboratory are the norm for those who want to succeed.

To avoid the demotivating effects of this lack of security on research scientists, the Wellcome Trust, the Lister Institute for Preventive Medicine and the Royal Society have schemes funding university research fellowships. Their aims are:

- to provide some support and freedom for young research scientists involved in postdoctoral work

- to encourage the cream of young British scientists to stay and work in Britain.

Although these high-flyers are a tiny minority of science graduates, their career development is vitally important to the science base in this country. The fact that some researchers take advantage of research opportunities overseas could be seen simply as an extension of the available job options, or might mean, as some suggest, that 'pure' scientific research is not valued in the UK. For more information on opportunities overseas, see Chapter seven.

Some researchers obtain more permanent employment with contract research organizations (The Association of Independent Research and Technology Organisations provides a list of these: www.airto. org.uk) or working for small research-based companies on science research parks (more details from the UK Science Parks Association: www.ukspa.org.uk).

Starting salaries – a postgraduate's bonus?

Advancement in some professional careers is not possible without further study, and most employers will pay a premium to graduates with a master's or other postgraduate qualification.

The average graduate starting salary is about £22,000 (2005). Employers are often prepared to pay around £2000 more for a PhD (DPhil) and £1000 more for an MSc or MA, although there is, of course, considerable variation, as there is among the starting salaries of graduates. Some employers pay over £3000 more, while others pay little extra. The figures, from the Association of Graduate Recruiters, refer to starting salaries in first jobs, and give no indication of future earning potential.

Making a choice

The science graduates in the profiles who did postgraduate studies had many different reasons for doing so. Mike Partridge (page 147) studied part-time for his PhD while working as a research scientist with Cranfield University. Sarah Polack wanted to further her interest in the public health of developing countries (page 168). Rachel McCoy (page 149) continued to research the subjects she became interested in as an undergraduate and eventually obtained her DPhil. Diana Robertson (page 130) wanted to teach. Mike Gilbert (page 185) needed to study at law school to become an intellectual property solicitor.

If you are interested in postgraduate study, you should start making applications very early in the final year of your undergraduate course. Information about opportunities is available through the careers services in universities and through university departments. If you are already in employment or applying for jobs you should also discuss the options with your (prospective) employer.

To summarise

■ In all, about a third of graduates in physics and chemistry are likely to do a higher degree or diploma immediately after their first degree. People with first-class degrees are even more likely to go on to further study.

■ More science graduates than arts or humanities graduates do higher degrees either full-time or part-time.

■ Computer science and engineering graduates are most likely to go straight into work.

■ About 2.7% of all science graduates go into teacher training. The employment prospects in teaching are good, particularly for science graduates.

■ Higher degrees are taken either by teaching or research.

■ Most employers pay a higher salary to new graduates with higher degrees, although the amount of the differential varies considerably.

Chapter seven
International opportunities

This chapter covers:

- the international nature of science
- studying abroad at different stages
- working abroad in different ways and in various countries
- the international community of scientific research
- the importance of language skills for work in the European Union.

Scientists abroad

UK nationals can live and work in any of the countries of the EU and the European Economic Area. Opportunities occur elsewhere in the world, but a visa will be required.

The international nature of science means there are many opportunities for science graduates to work or study overseas at some stage of their careers. One of the stated aims of the European Commission is to enhance the mobility of scientists between member states. The British Council promotes and strengthens Britain's achievements in science through its presence and activities in more than 100 countries throughout the world. It organises partnership programmes between British and European higher education, research institutions and laboratories and its website offers valuable insights into British science. Multinational organisations, such as oil companies, world trade and commerce all offer the chance to travel and work abroad.

Some young graduates choose short-term opportunities abroad while they have few responsibilities. Some want the chance to travel. Others may want to live and work abroad permanently.

Many young scientists in academic research find it difficult to get more than short-term contracts in Britain, so they are looking abroad. In the USA and, increasingly, in the rest of Europe, young British scientists are offered more job security, higher salaries and better funding for equipment. At the same time, many young scientists from other countries are coming to Britain for postgraduate and postdoctoral training before returning home. People also seek work abroad at a later stage in their careers because they feel that opportunities are limited in the UK.

Ways to go abroad

- All or part of an undergraduate course abroad

- A postgraduate course abroad

- Postdoctoral training overseas

- A permanent job in another country

- A job that takes you overseas

- Working for a multinational company, government and international organisations

- Casual work and volunteer projects

All or part of an undergraduate course abroad

Although students who want to study courses that are vastly oversubscribed and extremely competitive in the UK, such as veterinary science, can do so by finding a suitable course in another country, studying for a first degree at a university overseas is not a very practical idea for most people. There are numerous difficulties to overcome. Education systems in other countries are very different and courses can be much longer. You would have to find your living expenses and tuition fees, just as you would in the UK, and these vary considerably from one country to another. You also need to be fluent in the relevant language. This is not such a problem in English-speaking countries such as the USA, Canada or Australia, and even in the Netherlands some university courses are given in English.

In general, however, it is much easier to choose a degree course in the UK that allows you to spend time in a university overseas as part of your undergraduate studies. For example, Jane Antrobus spent the third year of a four-year environmental science and geography degree course in Australia, working as a voluntary research assistant in the Department of Tropical Environmental studies at James Cook University (page 133). There are various schemes that will enable you to pursue this option. A few courses lead to dual and triple awards. Many universities offer science courses which include a year of study in the USA. These are popular courses and get a lot of applicants.

The EU's Socrates-Erasmus programme promotes student mobility and cooperation in higher education in Europe. On the programme, students spend between three and twelve months studying in a European university on a programme which has been set up by their home university and which carries academic recognition. A Socrates-

Erasmus grant will cover travel and any living expenses over and above those which would have been incurred at home. Students who spend a full academic year on the programme do not have to pay tuition fees, either to their UK, or to the partner, institution. Those who spend less than twelve months will have to pay the full UK tuition fee to their home university (as applicable, according to their personal circumstances). Every year more than 8500 students from the UK participate in this programme, which covers 31 countries.

The Socrates-Erasmus programme also covers postgraduate study and there is a long list of affiliated university departments. Very often, these European links are for research degrees. The proportion of UK science graduates who go on to postgraduate study abroad is small for reasons much the same as for study abroad on a first degree course – the differences between the higher education systems, funding difficulties (there are some scholarships but most postgraduates fund themselves) and lack of language skills (institutions will require proof of some ability in the language of the host country).

If you are considering one of these programmes, it is vital to study the language of the country concerned to a standard which will allow you to understand lectures and tutorials and participate fully in student life. The Socrates-Erasmus programme can provide financial help with tuition in the language of the host country.

Finding a course

There are a number of undergraduate courses that will give you the chance to study languages as well as science. These could be combined courses in science and languages, but more often they are full science degree courses with language study alongside. Languages at A/AS level are not always required in order to do this kind of course, although clearly they would be a help. Many students complete their courses successfully with only a GCSE base in languages, but this does involve extra work.

Some students in applied science courses are lucky enough to be offered work experience overseas in their sandwich year. Taking time out of your university course for a work placement is common practice in many European countries: it is a way for employers to try out potential employees with no long-term commitment. These are called *stage* in France and *Praktikum* in Germany. Such placements are usually obtained through university departments. Some can be found through exchange programmes such as Leonardo da Vinci, which organises vocational training programmes in 30 European countries. The International Association for the Exchange of Students for Technical Experience (IAESTE) provides work placements for science and engineering students in more than 50 countries, most of which are during the summer vacation.

Information about Socrates-Erasmus courses can be found in *Experience Erasmus – the UK Guide* published by ISCO. Every year there are new schemes, and the details of the existing ones may change. You can also find out more from university departments and from university careers services. Many universities have Erasmus Clubs, sometimes run by the Students' Union, where participants get together and exchange experiences. There is now much more information available through all careers/Connexions services about studying and working in Europe.

A postgraduate course abroad

Some opportunities are available through UNESCO, which produces a book on study overseas, giving details of funding arrangements. Fellowships are scarce and applicants must have exceptional merit and outstanding potential. Scientists make up about a quarter of postgraduates taking UNESCO fellowships, with France and Germany being the countries taking most. Some people choose to study overseas after gaining some work experience here, for instance taking a management course in one of the European business schools.

Specialist master's courses began in the UK and are also available in many Commonwealth countries. Many of these courses in Australia and New Zealand have considerable numbers of British students, partly because there is no language barrier. The London based Association of Commonwealth Universities provides details of educational opportunities in the British Commonwealth.

Some master's courses have recently spread to European countries, most of them management-related. Knowledge of the local language is usually required except in the Netherlands, which has in recent years developed a range of postgraduate degrees that are presented in English.

Every year a number of young British science graduates go to the USA to do postgraduate training leading towards a doctorate. The structure of higher education is very different in the United States: graduate students start with a taught course before beginning their PhD research project, so you must be prepared to spend longer before getting a PhD than you would do in this country. You could even find yourself alongside American students who have graduated in other subjects, including humanities, and who are starting science at postgraduate level.

The Fulbright Commission, which has a London Office, provides advice on study in the USA, plus access to prospectuses. They also help students who are considering study in the USA to negotiate the application procedure, which usually includes passing an entrance test. The funding for postgraduate courses in the USA comes through each university department; in the private universities like Stanford and Yale, no particular preference is given to American students. The Fulbright Commission provides some scholarships for study in the USA but these are extremely competitive. A British student with a very strong academic record (minimum 2:1 degree) has a chance of being accepted. There are no subject restrictions and scholarships are offered for study at any approved university within the USA.

Postdoctoral training overseas

The most common way for young British research scientists to get experience abroad is at postdoctoral level. Short-term posts usually last two to three years, and are an excellent opportunity to broaden your experience and establish contacts in North American and European universities and research institutes – for instance, Mike Partridge (page 147) did postdoctoral research at Heidelberg University in Germany.

Grants and travel scholarships are provided by the funding bodies, including the Royal Society, the Wellcome Trust and NATO. Both the Royal Society and Wellcome Trust fund projects in Australia and New Zealand, many of which are concerned with health issues in the countries of South East Asia and the Pacific. Examples include investigations aimed at improving treatment for malaria and research designed to reduce death by pesticide poisoning in these developing countries.

A work permit is not required for the USA, although you must have a 'J-1' exchange visitor visa, which allows you to complete your fellowship.

If you want to take advantage of the international nature of research science, this may be a route for you. It is an opportunity that is peculiar to science postgraduates: it is almost unknown in other academic subjects.

Scientific research

In scientific research there are opportunities in 'intra-national' collaborative research laboratories, as well as in universities and research institutions. The Royal Society offers grants for study visits to and from the UK – maximum three months; fellowships to and from the UK – six to twelve months; and joint projects lasting up to three years. The Society is a founder member of the International Council for Science. Recent reports include those on carbon dioxide emissions, biological weapons controls, climate change, and infectious diseases in livestock. The Wellcome Trust offers a new collaborative research grants scheme with Australia and New Zealand, and supports researchers in 30 different countries. NATO supports international collaboration between scientists from countries of the Euro-Atlantic Partnership Council (EAPC). Its Security through Science programme is supporting research into defence against terrorism. The Department for International Development (DfID) also supports research in its quest to eradicate poverty. Currently, this includes work on HIV and tuberculosis in Africa, sustainable agriculture in developing countries and investigations into health problems experienced by mothers during pregnancy. In developing countries the risk of death during childbirth is dramatically higher than it is here.

Prestigious institutes compete to attract the best scientists no matter what their nationality, and they usually recruit people with a proven track record in their own country. Specialist skills can be a great advantage and scientists working in rapidly expanding areas of research, such as gene cloning, may suddenly find themselves very employable in other countries.

Sarah Polack

Sarah is working in medical research in Africa, and is particularly interested in the link between the environment and disease.

Career profile

Employer: London School of Hygiene and Tropical Medicine

Job title: research fellow

A levels: English, biology, geography

Degrees: BSc biological sciences, University of Liverpool
MSc: control of infectious diseases, London School of Hygiene and Tropical Medicine

'I took A levels in English, biology and geography. These choices were largely based on the subjects I had most enjoyed at GCSE level, and on a great interest in the environment and biology.

I then went on to do a degree in biological sciences at the University of Liverpool. It led to specialising in zoology in the final year. This course was well suited to me, geared to students who wish to study biology but are not yet certain which particular area they want to specialise in. Other options for specialisation included environmental biology, genetics, marine biology and microbiology. It was hard work, but a great course with a wide variety of unit options to select from. It is important to think early on, though, about what you may want to specialise in so that you take the necessary course options. Many of these units included field trips as well. In the first two years, four units were selected per term and these were assessed through coursework and examinations in January and May. In the final year core units were added, specific to the chosen honours degree.

Liverpool is a fun, lively and interesting city to live in. There are also plenty of things to get involved with at the university. I did a scuba diving course and was part of a group called 'Student Action for Refugees' (STAR). In hindsight, I wish I had got involved in these earlier during my degree as by the final year finding the time was harder.

As part of my degree, I took a course in parasitology run by the Liverpool School of Tropical Medicine. My final-year dissertation involved investigating women's ideas about health in pregnancy. Through these I developed a great interest in public health – an area that combined my interests in biology, disease and people.

Following my degree, in order to explore this interest in public health and epidemiology, I worked for a year at the University of Bristol, Department of Social Medicine. I was employed as a clerical assistant on health research projects and learned a great deal about what was involved in health research.

Through speaking to people both at Liverpool and Bristol University I learned about the London School of Hygiene and Tropical Medicine (LSHTM). I sent for a prospectus and found a number of courses that seemed really interesting and would enable me to further my interests and qualify me to work within the field of public health in developing countries. I then completed a one-year MSc in the control of infectious diseases, a course which aimed to bridge the disciplines of epidemiology, public health and laboratory sciences. The school is an amazing place to study, with great teaching and people from all over the world studying there. I am particularly interested in the link between the environment and disease and had the opportunity to become involved in the use of Geographical Information Systems (GIS) and its application to health.

Since completing my MSc, I have worked as a researcher at LSHTM on a number of projects, including a study of risk factors for highland malaria in Kenya; a study of the relationship between trachoma (an eye disease) and household access to water, and water use patterns in Tanzania; and a project to map the global distribution of trachoma using GIS. I am currently working on a project investigating the impact of cataract surgery on the quality of life and household economics in three countries – Kenya, Bangladesh and the Philippines. Currently a part-time member of staff, I am also a part-time PhD student and my present project is counting towards my PhD, which I hope to complete in three years' time. I think a science-based education is extremely valuable as it can lead you into so many different directions.'

Many academic scientists working in the UK have the opportunity to travel to conferences and make visits to other countries through their jobs.

A permanent job in another country

Is it really possible for new science graduates to get their first jobs overseas?

It happens, but is very unusual: only about 3% get permanent jobs abroad straight after graduation. Many more new graduates take temporary jobs, and of those finding permanent jobs overseas most do so later, after they have first gained experience from a UK base. At postgraduate level, the proportion working abroad straight away is higher, not including those doing postdoctoral fellowships.

There are a number of reasons why so few graduates get their first jobs overseas.

The difficulties

■ Higher education systems differ: degree courses are longer in the rest of Europe, so most new graduates from British universities, especially those on three-year degree courses, seem very young to European employers.

■ The language skills of British science graduates are poor in comparison with other Europeans: a lack of understanding of different cultures can also cause problems.

■ With improved higher education and training systems abroad, each country has graduates of its own and may well prefer to employ them. In non-EU countries, the employer would need to get a work permit for an employee who is not a citizen. This may prove difficult if there are suitable locals who can do the job. Unemployment exists outside the UK too!

■ Many countries have tightened their regulations regarding visas and recruitment.

■ A new graduate is unlikely to have much useful experience to offer. Employers in most European countries prefer to employ graduates with 'relevant' degrees. They also prefer those who have taken longer degrees, such as the four-year MSci, rather than the three-year BSc.

■ There are fewer jobs on the continent for which any degree would be acceptable, unlike the UK, where many administrative, trainee management and financial posts can be filled by any graduate.

Possible solutions

In spite of these difficulties, if you are determined and well prepared you may still succeed. There are always exceptions.

■ Improve your language skills: a knowledge of another European languages is a great asset if you want to live and work abroad.

■ If you have postgraduate qualifications, you are more likely to succeed.

- If you want to work overseas and do not have higher qualifications or contacts, it will pay you to get some job experience first so you have more to offer an employer.

- Links with companies through an exchange scheme, or through temporary work, a *stage* in France or a *Praktikum* in Germany, will give you an advantage.

- Join a British company that might offer the chance to work abroad later on, or apply to a multinational company with branches all over the world.

- You could join the Department for International Development. It recently introduced a recruitment scheme called the 'technical development' option. Applicants for the scheme must pass the Civil Service fast stream selection procedure, have postgraduate qualifications and have spent time in a developing country. Successful recruits will work directly on projects to assist developing countries through a range of options.

Where are the jobs?

Some European countries have shortages of trained scientists, as well as engineers and computer scientists. However, the opening up of Eastern Europe has altered the dynamics of the labour market in Europe and scientists from the East are now competing for jobs and training in the West. The increase in the number of countries in the European Union can only increase the opportunities. The European scientific information website www.cordis.lu is a good starting point for researching science in Europe.

There are opportunities for experienced staff in many African countries in agriculture, engineering, science teaching and other areas. There is some direct recruitment but this is mainly through UK-based organisations such as Crown Agents or the Department for International Development. Voluntary Service Overseas (VSO) also offers some opportunities.

Arab countries – particularly the major oil-producing countries that are undergoing economic expansion – advertise for staff in the

European press. They usually require senior managers and qualified professional staff who have experience related to the petrochemical or construction industries. Although attractive (tax-free) salaries are offered, it is important to consider carefully the implications of living and working in a country with a very different culture.

In Australia and Canada there may be less of a cultural difference but there are fewer opportunities. Because of the difficulties involved in obtaining work permits, only those foreigners with very specialised qualifications and experience have a chance, especially during an economic recession. A British-owned company in Australia would find the same obstacles to hiring a British scientist as a US-owned company would when trying to employ an American citizen in Malaysia. However, it is certainly possible for those under 27 years of age to go on a working holiday and have employment while they are there.

A job that takes you overseas

The UK is one of the world's foremost overseas investors and, for historic reasons, has commercial and cultural interests throughout the world. As a result, many British companies require their staff to work abroad for varying periods. Although improved communications mean fewer staff are now sent to live abroad permanently, an increasing number are going out for shorter periods from a UK base.

As large firms throughout Europe now see themselves as European, many are now recruiting graduates throughout the continent and establishing links for this purpose with universities in many EU countries. Many British companies are now keen to provide young workers with experience of working in different countries quite early in their careers.

Marketing and technical staff in particular are now more likely to be based in Britain and sent overseas on a regular basis. There are also increasing numbers of consultancies – in engineering, computing and finance, for example – and, more recently, in the transport, water treatment and communications industries. These firms are competing for work around the world, often working for government departments. Their staff are required to travel extensively, working on short-term projects in different countries. Drew Dewil, for example, a control engineer working with BP, works on the electronic systems required to control their operations in many different countries and regularly visits sites abroad from Alaska and Angola to Russia and Azerbaijan.

Business travel is usually highly structured and designed to fit in the maximum amount of work in the minimum time away from the home base. Your evenings may also be taken up with work-related activities and your weekends spent on planes, either moving on to the next destination or flying back home to start again on Monday morning. Travelling for work is far from a holiday: there are few opportunities to go sight seeing on a business trip. Scientists who travel to academic conferences, however, often find that the pace is more relaxed and can be combined with a few days' leisure.

Working for a multinational company

Many young graduates apply to join a multinational company in the hope that they will have the chance to travel and work overseas. The idea of working for a multinational may sound glamorous, but staff do not always have a great deal of choice about where they work or how much time they will spend outside the UK. The opportunity to travel depends on the nature of the business and the way the firm organises staff development and promotion.

Assignments vary too: a job in a Middle Eastern country is a very different proposition to a job in Europe. Language skills are always a great asset, no matter which country you visit, and can help you overcome some of the cultural differences that prevent many visitors from integrating into the local community. Language and cultural barriers often mean that social life is restricted to the company or an expatriate community within the 'host' country.

Spiralling costs have created numerous joint ventures between members of the European Union, and the aircraft industry is a good example of where engineers have found many employment opportunities in Europe. Paul Pilkington (see page 120) is a physics graduate working for Airbus and is employed on the aircraft testing side, which takes him to Toulouse in France.

Government and international organisations

A number of UK Government departments have opportunities for people who wish to travel and work for periods overseas. The Diplomatic Service, the Ministry of Defence, the Department for International Development and the Department of Trade and Industry are obvious examples. You might also consider the British Council and other international organisations such as the World Bank, the Organisation for Economic Cooperation and Development (OECD), the United Nations and its related organisations.

Then there are the European Union institutions and international collaborative projects, the European Patent Office and international research laboratories. European Patent Office staff regularly visit UK universities looking for recruits. Not all these organisations specifically recruit scientists, but many science graduates have a lot to offer. Although there are not many British science graduates working for them at present, there should be greater opportunities in the future. More and more often, the focus of international diplomacy and international relations is on technical and scientific problems. Well-trained and articulate people will be needed to solve them.

Casual work and volunteer projects

Before they decide on a particular career, many students are keen to spend some time after they finish their degree courses living and working abroad. If you would like to see more of the world in this way, there is a wide range of routes you can take. Lots of new graduates take short-term casual work, and scientists are no exception. You could experience life on a kibbutz in Israel, go to Australia on a 'young person's' visa, work in summer camps in the United States, help on an international work camp or take part in a project run by a group like Christians Abroad.

Voluntary organisations are usually looking for people with special skills and often ask for a longer-term commitment. In developing countries there are often opportunities for agriculture graduates, medical staff and engineers. New maths and science graduates are also sought for teaching jobs.

Voluntary Service Overseas (VSO) is the best known of these groups. VSO aims to promote and support human development through its work, to improve people's education and health, their income and employment opportunities, and their ability to contribute to the society in which they live. VSO volunteers, who usually go abroad for a two-year period, work alongside local people – teaching, sharing ideas and exploring different ways of working and training.

As a volunteer, you could end up working in a remote area so you need to be pretty self-reliant, although you will be thoroughly briefed in the UK before you go. Relevant work experience is in great demand, as most projects aim to provide local people with self-sufficiency and independence through practical training.

An overview

At every level, the international nature of science offers graduates a wide range of options.

If you decide to go into a scientific job you will be aware of scientific developments in other countries, from your first degree right through your career. You will communicate with other science specialists all over the world, through computer networks, the world wide web, conferences, visits, study and research projects overseas.

In scientific research there is an international community in each area of specialisation, and there are always opportunities for high flyers in laboratories and research institutes around the world. Science graduates go into many other jobs with an international dimension, involving travel or working for periods overseas. For most people, these opportunities come after first gaining some experience in the UK.

This may sound as if a science degree alone is a free ticket to travel the world, but there are other factors involved. Jobs abroad often require additional skills and experience and there will be keen competition from scientists in other countries. Having said that, there are many ways in which you can enhance your chances of working overseas.

British scientists have a distinct advantage in that English is the international language of science. However, although your scientific peers may understand written English and be able to conduct technical discussions, companies in Europe operate mostly in the language of the country where they are based. So for many science-related jobs and other careers that take you overseas, language skills are a great asset.

Many science graduates work overseas for some of their working lives, and some emigrate permanently, living and bringing up their families in a different culture. If the idea of an international career appeals to you, there are many ways in which you can prepare to become a world citizen. You'll have a high level of expertise in a field that is in demand, together with a working knowledge of at least one other major language, French, German or Spanish, for example, and the desire to experience a new way of life.

Chapter eight
Your future as a science graduate

This chapter covers:

■ where science graduates go after their first jobs

■ careers in research

■ changes in career development for science graduates

■ planning your moves

■ future demand for science graduates.

Vital statistics

As we have seen, the first destination statistics give only a limited view of the careers followed by science graduates. This book has shown you a selection of the wide range of first jobs, but these are just the starting points. People change jobs and develop in many different ways. For instance, more and more young graduates are taking temporary jobs or going on to further study.

Information on the career progression of science graduates is hard to obtain because people move around and the careers service loses touch with them. The employment situation changes very quickly, and surveys and statistics which you can refer to now may be completely out of date by the time you get to that stage. Alterations in corporate structures, economic and technological developments, political changes in Britain, continental Europe and the rest of the world are all factors that affect the supply of jobs and the lives of the people doing them. The people who are in senior positions today probably started out 30 or 40 years ago. Things were very different then, and they will have changed again by the time you get there. Above all, be flexible!

Scientists in Europe

There has been a growth in the numbers of research scientists and engineers in recent years, the largest numbers being in Germany, France and the UK. In fact, there is some evidence of oversupply. The UK is amongst those countries with the highest rate in proportion to the population.

Across Europe, there is some variation in the flexibility of occupational destinations of graduates according to their field of study. In Ireland and the UK, many jobs – over 50% of advertised vacancies – are open to graduates of any discipline, so many science graduates go into marketing and finance jobs, for example. However, this is not the case in other European countries, where the culture is more aligned to graduates entering careers that relate directly to their studies.

The position of graduates

Over the last 50 years there has been a downturn in graduate recruitment every ten years, usually at the start of each decade, while the later years of most decades have been buoyant. The first few years of this century saw a marked downturn in graduate recruitment. This was initially due to a cyclical economic downturn which followed the bursting of the e-bubble in 1999-2000, when many were investing in ultimately unprofitable internet-based companies. An immediate reduction in job prospects in computing and information technology followed which did not turn around until 2003. The decline was further exacerbated by subsequent events, especially the impact of terrorism in September 2001.

This led to a major decline in the American economy, which in turn affected the rest of the world. Since 2003, however, the graduate labour market has improved dramatically. Between 2004 and 2005 graduate vacancies increased by 11%. However, demand for graduates declined in the pharmaceutical, chemical and water industries and jobs for new graduates in scientific research and development fell by 18%.

In 2005, the median graduate salary in the UK was £22,000. Graduates in science received £21,000 on average, with the figures for those with civil (£21,000) and electrical engineering (£20,800) degrees being similar, and those with chemical engineering slightly higher (£24,000). Rates in London were significantly higher than elsewhere, averaging £4500 more than the rest of England and £8000 more than in Wales and Northern Ireland. Graduates with master's degrees, and those who have been sponsored through their degree by an employer, tend to be paid above the average, but only to the tune of around £1000 p.a. The pay of those with doctorates averages around £2000 more, but it has to be remembered that it takes three years of research after an undergraduate degree to reach that situation.

Management level

It has been a concern that science graduates could get stuck in research and development posts, and not become as dominant in top management in the UK as they are abroad. Most young science graduates join large companies straight into a specific job, whereas others join a general management training programme that often involves working in different areas of the company. Science graduates can find themselves cut off from the rest of the company, while others are more aware of the whole organisation, which gives them an advantage when it comes to promotion up the management ladder. Many science-based companies have a dual ladder scheme, where you can choose to develop your career within management or as a technical specialist. Leading recruiters of scientists have fast-track graduate management training schemes.

However, graduates are now much better represented further down the corporate hierarchy, so, in the fullness of time, the balance should change further up. Science graduates starting in research work can also progress into other science-related activities as their careers develop. The choices vary, depending on the industry and the particular company you are working for. Many scientists with postgraduate degrees, especially doctorates, make their careers in consultancies where their problem-solving and communication skills are used to the full. These are often scientific, environmental or engineering consultancies but also include firms in management and financial consultancy.

Andy Malone

At school Andy was not sure whether geography or physics was his favourite subject. In the end he decided to study physics at university. He discovered that in some physics degree courses geology was an option and chose the natural sciences tripos at Cambridge. This was flexible enough to allow him to start by studying physics but end up with a geology degree.

Career profile

Job title: geoscientist

Employer: BP

A levels: physics, geography, maths, further maths

Degree: natural sciences

University: Cambridge

'I was 14, and making choices about what to study at GCSE, when I first became conscious of my leaning towards sciences.

During the next two years I found that I had an aptitude for physics, chemistry, maths and geography, my favourite subjects. My A level choices reflected this scientific bias – I plumped for double maths, physics and geography. Maths was something I could do well, but it seemed pretty uninspiring to me. I enjoyed physics, as it seemed to get to the heart of everything and explain how the world worked, but it was geography that was my real passion. The most enjoyable but also the hardest A level, the focus was on physical geography, as reflected in my choice of project – a study on footpath erosion that accounted for 20% of the final marks. I started looking at university courses and decided to apply for a physics degree. I couldn't see where geography might lead, and I was keen to keep getting to the bottom of things with physics. As I looked around I discovered that several physics courses included geology as an optional subject; this seemed the ideal route for me to indulge certain aspects of my physical geography background at university.

Eventually I chose a natural sciences degree at Cambridge, which is an extremely flexible course. I made the required A level grades, and in my first year studied physics, geology, maths and computer science. I got high marks in physics but was starting to become disillusioned with it; the subject had changed so much from A level. Maths and computer science failed to capture my imagination, but geology was superb. I found it hugely enjoyable, was good at it, and so it was the natural choice for me to specialise in for the following years.

I studied a broad selection of geology, including geophysics, tectonics, hard and soft rocks and palaeontology. The courses were interesting and well constructed, the Earth Sciences department friendly and the fieldwork was a real bonus. After my BA I stayed on to do a master's degree, including a thesis on earthquake seismology.

It was during my master's year that I started to think seriously about my career. I toyed with the idea of management consulting because I've always been into figuring out why things don't work and how they might be improved. But ultimately I did not want to drop everything I'd learned during my degrees.

I looked at a career in oil and gas and went to BP for a geoscience internship in Aberdeen, immediately after finishing my master's. It proved to be a very valuable summer. I began to understand where and how my geoscience skills could be used in a career, as well as becoming aware of the gaps in my knowledge that I would have to plug. It also gave me my first taste of the global oil business. BP provided a very supportive environment with excellent training and logistics, social events and plenty of opportunities for networking.

Now I'm a development geoscientist with BP, working on oilfields whose production behaviour needs to be understood and managed. My job includes building reservoir models for North Sea fields: I integrate geological and geophysical data to form as accurate a description as possible of the reservoir's 3-D rock and fluid properties. This forms the basis for the reservoir engineer's simulation models. I am also involved in planning new seismic acquisition.

It's a steep learning curve, involving getting to grips with not only specialist petroleum geoscience, but also the upstream oil and gas industry as a whole. Integration with other disciplines is key, including understanding commercial drivers, targets and metrics. I am well supported by my colleagues and training, and am enjoying learning and implementing new skills in this challenging environment.

The lifestyle suits me well. I start work around 8.00 and finish by 5:30. Living in Aberdeen is great if you're into the outdoors. I cycle to work, and am so close to the hills that I get frequent fixes of mountain biking and hill walking.

The city has a good social scene, and working nine-day fortnights means I'm not short of long weekends.

Progression from research into other science-related activities might include the following options:

- Research management

- Development work

- Project management

- Production management

- Quality assurance

- Marketing – market assessment

- Technical sales

- Licensing of intellectual property

- Commercial development

- Information technology

- Patent agent

- Human resources – recruiting and training scientists.

All of these activities can lead you into middle and then senior management. Once again the move is usually from specialist jobs to generalist positions, rather than the other way round. Science graduates are generally unlikely to start in marketing and move into research and development, or to start in human resources and move into production. People with scientific and technical specialisms have to learn new skills in areas like management, finance, commerce and marketing.

Mike Gilbert

Mike's experience demonstrates that you can use your science degree to move into a very different career, but it often helps if you pick up other skills, such as negotiating and organising, quite early in your career – perhaps, as in his case, when still a student.

186 | Careers with a Science Degree

Career profile

Job title: intellectual property solicitor

Employer: Marks and Clerk Solicitors (specialising in intellectual property)

A levels: maths, physics, chemistry, further maths

Degree: natural sciences (chemical engineering)

University: Cambridge

'When I was at school, I had my heart set on becoming a research physicist, probably largely due to my dad's influence (surprisingly, he was a research physicist) though, to be fair, I was also inherently interested in the subject. I chose maths, physics, chemistry and further maths A levels. In addition, I took special papers in maths and physics. When I was in the sixth form, I applied to Cambridge University to read natural sciences (physical) because I thought that Cambridge had one of the best reputations for teaching science in the country. I was duly accepted following a conditional offer. However, midway through my first year, it dawned on me that physics may not be the be all and end all. I found that, at university, the emphasis was on academic research. Nevertheless, Cambridge opened my horizons and gave me so many new opportunities that I had not had before.

In my third year, having taken the chemical engineering options of the natural sciences tripos, I decided that I did not want to pursue a career in science but equally, I did not want to waste all the years of my scientific education.

At that time, I was appointed as the president of my college student union. I enjoyed representing student views and opinions to the college and university governing bodies. During discussions with the university careers service, I was asked if I had considered converting to law and specialising in intellectual property. After some digging around, I discovered that intellectual property covered the law of ideas, including patents, trade marks, copyrights and industrial designs. This sounded an ideal blending of what I perceived were my two main strengths – an understanding of science and technology and an ability to represent people.

Before taking matters further, I decided that I first needed to secure funding for my legal education. I approached a number of leading firms of solicitors specialising in the field and very quickly obtained two years' funding for my academic courses and an offer of a two-year training contract. Trainee solicitors without a degree in law must complete two years at law school followed by two years' training (known as a training contract) in a solicitor's office. Luckily, I was offered a place to stay on at Cambridge for a fourth year to do the Common Professional Examination (CPE), now often called the postgraduate diploma in law. This is the qualification which can lead to a career either as a barrister or a solicitor. I then moved to Nottingham Law School to study the Legal Practice Course as it is now called.

I found that studying law was very rewarding and a wholly different experience from studying science! I moved to London in 1991 and qualified as a solicitor in 1993. I rapidly became heavily involved in highly scientific cases concerning pharmaceutical patent disputes, chemical patent matters, industrial espionage and breach of confidence cases. All of these cases have involved me using the scientific knowledge I have built up over the years.

I am now a partner in a firm of solicitors which specialises in intellectual property law. I continue to use my scientific training, which has proved to be invaluable in my choice of career. Currently, I intend to stay in private practice as I enjoy the variety of work and client contact. My career shows that a science degree can give you a very solid background for a career in law, and I would recommend this to any prospective lawyer, even if they were not considering specialising in intellectual property.'

Career progression and hierarchy

There have been changes made to the structure of businesses over recent years which have been welcomed by science graduates.

■ Organisations have become less hierarchical, and layers of middle management have gone.

■ More specialists, who have been educated to a high level, are needed.

■ To advance your career, you do not have to climb the organisational ladder.

■ Graduates are assuming more positions of responsibility than before.

When you are hired as a scientist you may join a project team where using and developing your scientific skills is an essential aspect of your work. Hierarchical management systems, where people report up a management line from the bottom to the top, have been largely replaced by matrix management methods in which people from several different disciplines work together to combine their knowledge in order to solve problems more quickly. It is essential in such environments to have the ability to explain your science – not only to scientists but also, without jargon, to those who have little understanding of scientific principles.

Career progression in industrial science often leads to being a project leader, first of small projects and subsequently of larger ones. Inevitably, it eventually becomes necessary to develop one's management skills, adding responsibility for budgets, training and supervising staff, liaising with external people or organisations that have an interest in the work. So career development leaves less time for bench science and requires more time for setting goals, deciding priorities and the direction of investigations. An important part of this is interpreting results, perhaps in relation to business and commercial requirements as well as scientific ones.

As their careers move on many scientists take on other roles as described earlier in this chapter. Their ever-widening skills base, with management skills in addition to the purely technical ones, increases their employability. Provided that they are flexible and adaptable, science graduates can look forward to excellent, satisfying careers. There is a danger in research-related jobs that some scientists become more and more focused and increasingly specialised. If they see their career in terms of a highly specialist area of science rather than the skills that they gain from working in science, they may neglect to develop their wider skills, become less flexible and adaptable than other employees and take their careers into a cul-de-sac. With careful thought and a little career planning this can easily be avoided.

Planning your moves

The difficult thing for young scientists is to decide when the time is right to move out of research, if this is what they eventually wish to do. There is a danger of leaving it too late. It is very difficult as a new graduate to know which way your skills and interests might lead you at different stages of your career. Research in industry attracts a very different individual from the one who prefers development work – turning ideas into potential products, overseeing pilot production, testing and scaling up. Development work includes not only the science but also assessing the safety and economic value of new products and services. Some science graduates get more interested in development work later on in their careers, but others decide to move into quite different areas.

A crucial element of career planning is avoiding the cul-de-sac, unless, of course, it is one you are particularly happy in. Being able to move to other areas, using your expertise in a different setting, learning new skills, having the chance to try new roles – these all seem more desirable in a career than edging up predetermined structures and waiting around for 'dead men's shoes'.

And you have plenty of expertise already. There are many skills that you can acquire through academic study, and through working in scientific research and development, which are easily transferable to other career areas, and much in demand.

- Numeracy – scientific disciplines involve working with numerical data at a level which is acceptable for most jobs. The ability to complete statistical analyses is an advantage.

- Communication – scientists are adept at writing reports and presenting their results verbally.

- Thoroughness and accuracy

- Problem solving

- Self-motivation

- Organisation and time management

- Team skills

- Information technology skills

Responsibility for your career planning is, ultimately, your own, although many companies encourage their staff to think of career progression outside research and development as well as within it.

Industry is not the only option

Not all science graduates want to run large industries or stalk the corridors of power. Many want to work in some aspect of science because it interests them and they feel it is worthwhile. They feel they can make important contributions to the development of knowledge, to education, to the application of science to problems for the benefit of our own standard of living and economy, as well as to global problems such as poverty, hunger and the environment.

Some science graduates see themselves as scientists all their working lives. Others use their scientific training to become managers, teachers, librarians, charity field workers, publishers, agricultural advisers, actuaries or patent agents. Different roles suit different people at different stages of their careers: the job you choose early on in your career may not be the right one in a few years' time. By staying flexible and maintaining your transferable skills you can give yourself more options when the time comes to reassess your situation at work.

There continues to be a severe shortage of science teachers in secondary schools, particularly in physics and chemistry, and a lack of scientists entering teacher training courses. Also, unusually large numbers of science teachers are currently aged 45-54 and shortly to retire.

Where will the jobs be?

In academic science, shortages are predicted. If young academics are not recruited now, there will be unfilled vacancies in higher education when the present generation retires. There will be a continuing demand from the schools and from further education as the importance of science and technical education is more fully realised.

The general public's increasing interest in science and science-related issues means more opportunities for science graduates in the media and in communications. The continual growth of scientific knowledge requires explanation and interpretation: this will lead to jobs in areas like specialist communications, information science/management and technical publishing.

Information technology will continue to dominate communications at all levels of industry, commerce and public and private life. Again scientists are in a strong position to find opportunities here. The IT knowledge and experience gained on your degree course will be a great asset in all sorts of jobs and will give you a real advantage over less IT-literate graduates at all levels.

The internationalisation of science-based companies will continue to increase opportunities in the EU and further afield. Opportunities will continue to be offered in developing countries where growth depends on scientific expertise. The peculiarly British phenomenon of having few scientists in top government and management posts may be changed by influence from countries that are more successful in science-related industries.

In the near future, science graduates may find themselves in increasing demand because the proportion of people studying science is not keeping pace with the general rise in the number of graduates.

Competition for jobs that require a science degree will not be as high, and the articulate and literate science graduate may have a scarcity value when applying for the whole range of other jobs open to graduates of any discipline.

In summary

- Continuing changes in graduate employment mean that what happened to those who left higher education in the past is not necessarily relevant to you today.

- Opportunities for science graduates are increasing due to rapid developments in many areas: science, technology, communications, company structures, international relations and global markets.

- Science graduates (including doctors) have a wider choice of jobs overseas than other graduates.

- Science graduates have an important part to play in many areas of work. To take advantage of all the options on offer, you need to complement your qualifications in science and IT with a range of skills in communication.

- An increasing recognition of the importance of science to the prosperity of this country should mean better opportunities for science graduates in the future.

Chapter nine
Where do you go from here?

This chapter covers:

- taking stock of where you are
- planning your next step
- sources of information and advice
- events you can look out for
- action you can take.

Your career, your decision

This final chapter is about what you
can do now to help yourself take decisions, make progress and turn your plans into reality. You will find lots of suggestions of things to do, people to talk to and information to use. You need to think about your own interests and preferences as well as look at the different options that are available.

If all this sounds like a lot of hard work, remember it is vitally important to you. You will find so much of your time gets taken up with all the short-term issues: this week's homework, next week's concert or party, the next match, holidays or exams at the end of the year. Your degree and career choices are much more important in the long term and really deserve your attention. It is your future and only you can make it work.

Start from where you are now

The sections below will give you useful leads. If you have already started your A levels, Highers or BTEC National course, skip Stage 1 and go straight to Stage 2.

Stage 1 – Choosing A levels, BTEC National or Advanced Highers

Start thinking and planning at the end of year 10 and the very beginning of year 11. Use some of your holiday period too! Look at the lists below. Plan how you could achieve these aims.

Consider all your options

- Use the careers library.

- Use occupational information databases.

- Read *Which A levels?*

- Look at all the courses on offer.

- Get prospectuses from local colleges and sixth forms.

- Visit open days.

- Talk to your teachers.

- Talk to sixth-form and college staff.

- Look at *What Do Graduates Do?*

Decide what really matters to you

- Talk to your family and friends.

- Talk to your personal/careers adviser.

- Use computer guidance programmes.

- Try to get work experience or do work shadowing.

- Attend lectures and visits, science fairs and science conventions.

- Read *New Scientist* and science articles in the press.

- Watch programmes like *Rough Science, The Sky at Night, Horizon*, and the many excellent natural history programmes. The Discovery channel offers many science-related programmes too.

Work-related qualifications which can lead on to degree courses

A levels in applied subjects

A levels in applied subjects (such as applied science, applied ICT and engineering) are widely accepted for entry onto higher education courses, although an accompanying A level in maths or a single subject science may be required. A levels in applied subjects have a different approach from other A levels, with much more project work. A double award (12 units) is equivalent to two A levels or a BTEC National Certificate.

BTEC National qualifications

BTEC National Certificates and Diplomas can also lead on to degree courses. The 12-unit Certificate is the equivalent of two A levels and is widely accepted by HE institutions, although an accompanying A level in maths or a single subject science may be required. Distinctions or merits are generally required. The 18-unit Diploma is the equivalent of three A levels. BTEC National qualifications are mostly college-based and last for two years, full time.

Maths (again!)

Take stock of your maths. For further study in science, maths is a vitally important tool. Even if you are not intending to study maths for A level, you should try to take it as far as you can. You could take AS level maths alongside other level 3 studies.

Using careers software

There are literally dozens of careers software products on the market and, with the increasing availability of information on the internet, there are arguably more 'attractive' and more popular ways for you to access careers information than ever before. There is no one program on the market which will satisfy all users from age 15 upwards, so choose one which is most appropriate for the stage you are at in your education.

Occupational information databases

They offer quick and easy access to:

■ work details

■ entry routes and training given

■ personal qualities and skills checklists

■ similar job areas

■ professional bodies to write to

■ higher education information

■ addresses for further information

■ references for further exploration.

Examples of this sort of database include:

■ *Prospects*

■ *KeyCLIPS* from Lifetime Careers Publishing

■ *CID* from Careersoft

■ *Explorer 2000* from JIIG-CAL Progressions Ltd

■ *Kudos*, *Careerscape* and *Careersphere* from CASCAiD

■ *Odyssey* from Progressions Ltd.

Most of these have easy-to-use searching routes, enabling you to match your subject interests, perceived skills and personal interests to career ideas.

Careers guidance and self-assessment software

This will help you become aware of your own occupational interests. Most will ask you to complete an interest questionnaire or guide. Your responses will be matched to a database of occupations, with most programs giving you an option to see the pros and cons (positive and negative aspects) of any job on the list.

Examples of this sort of guidance software include:

- *Pathfinder* from JIIG-CAL Progressions Ltd

- *Prospects Planner*

- *Kudos* and *Adult Directions* from CASCAiD

- *Iscom* and *Iscope* from ISCO

- *ProMICAD* from Lifetime Careers Publishing

To search for, and identify, relevant courses of study

Use databases of further and higher education. Information can be accessed by full-time/part-time/correspondence/geographical location/A level points and so on. Gateways to the internet are also possible on some programs.

Examples of this sort of software include:

- *Studylink* from UCAS

- *Course Discover* from Trotman

- *Higher Ideas* from Careersoft

- *Discourse* from ISCO.

To investigate work and study opportunities in Europe and beyond

These can be accessed through a number of software programs. You should not underestimate the potential growth of jobs in scientific and technical occupations that are available in Europe and worldwide.

Some programs which could help you include:

- *Europe in the Round* from Vocational Technologies Ltd
- *EXODUS* from Careers Europe.

The media

New Scientist is a weekly science magazine available in newsagents, local libraries and many schools. It has lots of news about developments in sciences and some careers articles as well. *Focus* is a science magazine that is published monthly. *Scientific American* has much longer in-depth articles about scientific topics but can be understood by A level students. Other useful magazines include *Nature* and *Science*. Reading about science and watching TV science programmes will also help you to identify where your scientific interests lie.

Stage 2 – Choosing a science degree

You should be planning and thinking soon after you start your post-16 study. So you need to start straight away. Set some of your summer holiday aside for this!

Consider all your options

- Use your Connexions/careers library.
- Use computer databases.
- Look at *Which Degree? Sciences* (published by Hobsons).
- Read the CRAC *Degree Course Guides* (published by Trotman).
- Visit higher education conventions and fairs.

- Go to open days.

- Go on introductory courses in universities, e.g. WISE (Women into Science and Engineering).

- Look at *What Do Graduates Do?* (published by AGCAS).

- Look at *Graduate Career Guides – Science* (published by Hobsons).

- Read the brief descriptions of the main science subjects offered at universities in the Glossary on page 219.

Decide what really matters to you

- Talk to friends and family.

- Talk to your personal adviser.

- Talk to your teachers.

- Try to do some work experience or work shadowing.

- Use computer-based guidance systems.

- Use computer-based HE choice systems.

- Talk to scientists you meet.

Alternative courses

Don't forget you could do a sandwich course or get work experience as part of your degree course. You might also consider a course with a European link or one which will give you the chance to study or work overseas.

Alternative qualifications

Remember there is a whole range of Higher National Diploma courses with entry requirements of one A level pass or equivalent. This could be a good alternative to a degree course if you feel the required grades are too high for you, or you prefer the more applied vocational nature of an HND course. Two-year full-time foundation degrees are offered in work-related subjects and can be taken on a part-time basis, appealing to those who wish to study whilst in employment.

Yet another route is to go straight into employment as an advanced apprentice. After two years you can attain a National Vocational Qualification. This can be acceptable for entry onto a foundation degree. Success in a foundation degree can then lead to acceptance on an honours degree course. But be aware that this is a very long route to a science degree and may not be acceptable to some employers.

Work experience and work shadowing

Many schools have work experience programmes in year 10 or year 11 which give you the chance to work in an organisation and find out about the jobs people do. If you are in the sixth form you may also be able to do work experience, but on a very part-time basis or in the holidays.

Work shadowing is when you spend a day or two following someone doing a particular job, watching them at work, and seeing and hearing about the job at first hand. This is often a good way to get to know about the tasks involved in higher-level jobs which you would be less likely to be able to try out on work experience. Ask your school or college careers/personal adviser or your science teachers about these schemes. Girls who would like to meet, or shadow, women science or engineering graduates can make contact through the local branch of WISE. Ask your science teachers to help you.

Higher education conventions

Many Connexions/careers services and UCAS run events where you can meet representatives from universities and colleges from all over the country who will tell you about their courses. You can also get information about career opportunities after courses. These are well worth attending, particularly if you have done some preparatory work first, and have prepared questions to ask and interests to follow up. You will also be able to get information about course fees, student finance and sponsorships. The Department for Education and Skills website on student support, www.dfes.gov.uk/studentsupport also includes much valuable financial information.

Open days

Lists of open days in universities and colleges should be available in your school. Some are for all students, others are for students interested in particular subjects, e.g. sciences or engineering. Ask your careers teacher for information.

'Taster' courses

Some universities and other organisations run courses of up to a week for students interested in specific courses. Again your school or college will have information.

Reference books

There are many reference books about higher education and the courses on offer. These will be available in your school or college careers library, in the careers/Connexions centre or local public library. See the Book list for more details.

Stage 3 – Moving on from your degree or diploma course

This stage may be a long way in the future, but the process is the same as for Stages 1 and 2. The skills you learn now in researching options and using careers information will help you through Stage 3 too.

You would start thinking and planning Stage 3 in your second year on a three-year course, or the third year if you are on a four-year course.

Consider all your options

- Use your university or college careers service.

- Read *What Do Graduates Do?*

- Look at the AGCAS publication *Your Degree ... What Next?*

- Look at the website of the professional body that relates to your degree – e.g. Institute of Physics.

■ Investigate www.prospects.ac.uk for occupational information.

■ Talk to your tutors and lecturers.

■ Attend careers events, skills workshops and employers' presentations.

■ Investigate internships during the autumn term of your penultimate year – some employers recruit graduates via this route.

■ Talk to employers at career fairs and while on work experience or holiday jobs.

■ Keep reading the science magazines.

Decide what really matters to you

■ Talk to university or college careers advisers.

■ Use computer-based guidance systems such as *Prospects Planner*.

■ Talk to your lecturers about your work.

■ Talk to postgraduate students.

■ Seek out people doing jobs you are interested in.

■ Use the internet to investigate companies and vacancies.

■ Investigate employer details on trade association and professional body websites.

For women

Seek out your local WISE group and attend their meetings. Investigate the websites specifically designed for women wishing to progress their careers in science and technology (see 'Women' in the useful addresses section).

Postgraduate courses

Don't forget there are all sorts of different ways of getting postgraduate qualifications.

They can be taken immediately after your first degree, but also later while you are at work or after some work experience. There are part-time as well as full-time courses.

Details of postgraduate courses can be found on www.postgrad. hobsons.co.uk and www.prospects.ac.uk. Funding for postgraduate study can sometimes be obtained from the Research Councils, medical charities and employers.

Careers services

Universities and colleges of higher education have careers services where you can have access to an information library, computer databases, vacancy information, computer-aided guidance, aptitude tests and personal guidance from a careers adviser. You can also discover from them which employers recently recruited graduates from your course. Careers services have links with employers who habitually recruit from your university. Investigate these.

Careers fairs

Your careers service will organise presentations by employers about their companies, as well as general talks on careers topics. There may also be careers fairs, with many employers looking to recruit suitable graduates. This is where you can go and meet employers informally.

Holiday jobs

Science graduates are particularly successful at getting vacation work, sometimes in laboratories. This experience will give you a financial boost but will also provide some insights into how attractive you find certain jobs and how you would fit in at work.

Careers courses

Full-time graduate students have the chance to participate in the UK Graduate Programme – www.grad.ac.uk. This provides personal skills development opportunities for postgraduate students through a programme of national residential courses lasting three, four or five days. The programme is supported by the Research Councils.

Further study

If you are interested in further academic study then talk to your tutors and lecturers. They will have many contacts with other departments and research groups. You will need to get information about funding too.

Investigating other issues raised in this book

The sections above have covered ways of finding out about the range of options open to you at each stage and how you can get help with your decision making. But you might also want to investigate further some of the important issues we have raised about science and science careers before making your choices.

You might want to follow up the issues of image, status, gender and career development. There is some factual information available on these topics, but you will also come across a great deal of opinion and strongly-held views. Take care to apply the same rigorous scrutiny to these that a scientist would apply to a scientific question!

In your research you will need to examine lots of different sources and talk to many different people. Try to relate the opinions you hear to the experiences of the people you are talking to. What is their standpoint? You will need other points of view to get a balanced picture. Allow for human error and then talk to a few more people.

You will also want to think about how the information will affect you. Will you have the same experience? Do you have the same concerns? How will you avoid the pitfalls and make the best of the opportunities? Bear in mind that things are constantly changing.

You will meet useful people to talk to through everyday student life, by using the careers guidance services, through holiday jobs and work experience, and through your friends and family. Get in touch with professional associations, such as the Institute of Biology, and local firms. It is surprisingly easy to find the contacts – what takes more initiative is to ask people for some of their time and make good use of it.

You will find that most people will be happy to talk to you about their work and how they got into it. Sometimes the only problem is stopping them talking! If you are well prepared with questions on issues that are important for you, they will be glad to give you the time. A word of warning: beware of people who offer you directive advice! They are usually thinking of themselves, not you. Advice that begins, 'If I were you ...' usually means 'I wish I had done this.' They may be trying to be helpful but the right decision for them would not necessarily suit you.

Whatever stage you are at, make yourself a plan of action. Make a list of things you have to do to get all the information, advice and experience you need to give you a solid base for your next decision point. Make a list and a timetable of actions. Then make sure you follow it up. It helps if you give yourself target dates and get a friend to check your progress. It's your future and only you can make the decisions, so put yourself firmly in charge.

And finally

This book has tried to give a positive but realistic picture of career opportunities with a science degree. An education in science is not a panacea for all. The bad news is that science has, in some respects, a poor image. Scientists often feel they have low status and that they get unfairly blamed for some of today's problems. Science graduates are not yet in enough of the very top jobs; research scientists are struggling for funding and a clear career structure; many women scientists feel that science is still a man's world. The good news, on the other hand, is that a science education will help you to understand and contribute to many of the most important issues of the 21st century. You will have knowledge and experience that can be applied in many different work situations, scientific and non-scientific, in the UK and overseas. You will be well equipped to deal with the information

gy revolution, and you will have an international outlook
late for the important challenges of the future. Together
ner young science graduates, male and female, in all sorts of
nt roles, you can make a difference. Go for it!

inal comment comes from the school report of one of the most
ous scientists of all time. It's worth remembering when you hit a
icult patch in your studies or career.

e will never amount to anything.'

Having almost failed his degree course, Albert Einstein went on to
be a teacher, patent agent and finally a Nobel prizewinning research
scientist.

Booklist

Some of these books may be in your school, college, Connexions/ careers service or public library. See also the computer programs and databases listed in Chapter nine.

Careers using science, technology or mathematics

Career Guides series includes: *Science & IT, Engineering* – published annually by Hobsons

Engineering and Technology; Chartered Patent Attorneys; Information Technology – titles published annually by Inside Careers

Engineering, Healthcare Professions and *IT and the Internet* – titles in the *Getting into* series, published by Trotman

Who wants to be a scientist? Choosing science as a career – by Nancy Rothwell, published by Cambridge University Press

Choosing A level and equivalent courses

Which A Levels? – published by Lifetime Careers Publishing

How to Choose your A-Levels – published by Trotman

Choosing a science degree

Which Degree Volume 2: engineering, technology, geography, sciences, medicine, mathematics – published annually by Hobsons

CRAC Degree Course Guides – (covering individual subject areas) published biennially by Trotman

University and College Entrance: The Official Guide – published annually by UCAS (with detailed entry requirements on accompanying CD ROM)

Guides series includes: *Computer Science Courses, Engineering Healthcare Professions Courses* and *Physical Sciences Courses* ned annually by UCAS/Trotman

y of University and College Entry (DUCE) – published annually ,tman

e Course Offers – published annually by Trotman

erience Erasmus: the UK Guide – published annually by the ISCO ιe Independent Schools Careers Organisation)

on't forget to use course databases and websites too, such as ,CCTIS UK *Course Discover* and the UCAS website www.ucas.com ）r *Exodus* from Careers Europe.

Postgraduate courses and destinations

What Do Graduates Do? – published annually by Graduate Prospects

What Do PhD Graduates Do? – published by UK Grad

Funding

www.dfes.gov.uk/studentsupport

Grants Register – published by Palgrave Macmillan

Directory of Grant Making Trusts – published by the Charities Aid Foundation

Publishers' addresses and websites

Lifetime Careers Publishing – titles available from Orca Book Services Ltd, Stanley House, 3 Fleets Lane, Poole BH15 3AJ. Tel: 01202 665432. www.lifetime-publishing.co.uk

Trotman Publishing – titles available from Plymbridge Distributors Ltd, Plymbridge House, Estover Road, Plymouth PL6 7PZ. Tel: 0870 900 2665. www.career-portal.co.uk

Hobsons Publishing – titles are available from Plymbridge Distributors Ltd, Plymbridge House, Estover Road, Plymouth PL6 7PZ. Tel: 01752 202301. www.hobsons.co.uk

Graduate Prospects – Prospects House, Booth Street East, Manchester M13 9EP. Tel: 0161 277 5200. www.prospects.ac.uk

ISCO Publications – 12A Princess Way, Camberley, Surrey GU15 3SP. Tel: 01276 21188. www.isco.org.uk

UCAS Distribution – PO Box 130, Cheltenham GL52 3ZF. Tel: 01242 544610. www.alphabookstore.com/ucas/

A good science read

The Universe in a Nutshell – by Stephen Hawking, published by Bantam

Brief History of Time – by Stephen Hawking, and *A briefer History of Time* – by Stephen Hawkins and Leonard Mlodinow, both published by Bantam

A Short History of Nearly Everything – by Bill Bryson, published by Black Swan

DNA: The Science of Life – by J.D. Watson, published by Arrow

Genes, Girls and Gamow – by J.D. Watson, published by Oxford University Press

Darwin's Watch: Science of Discworld III – by Terry Pratchett, Ian Stewart, Jack Cohen, published by Ebury Press

The Science of Discworld – by Terry Pratchett, Ian Stewart, Jack Cohen, published by Ebury Press

The Science of Discworld II: The Globe – by Terry Pratchett, Ian Stewart, Jack Cohen, published by Ebury Press

Galileo's Daughter: a drama of science, faith and love – by Dava Sobel, published by Fourth Estate

*What the Victorians Did for U*s – by Adam Hart-Davis, published by Headline Books

Rocket Man: Robert H. Goddard and the Birth of the Space Age – by David Clary, published by Hyperion

The Selfish Gene – by Richard Dawkins, published by Oxford Paperbacks

Space: our Final Frontier – by John Gribbin, published by BBC Books

Does God Play Dice? The New Mathematics of Chaos – by Ian Stewart, published by Penguin

The Big Questions in Science – edited by Harriet Swain, published by Cape

The Skeptical Environmentalist – by Bjorn Lomborg, published by Cambridge University Press

Rosalind Franklin: The Dark Lady of DNA – by Brenda Maddox, published by HarperCollins

Aeons: The Search for the Beginning of Time – by Martin Gorst, published by HarperCollins

A Question of Trust: the BBC Reith Lectures 2002 – by Onora O'Neill, published by Cambridge University Press

Fermat's Last Theorem – by Simon Singh, published by Fourth Estate Ltd

Useful addresses, telephone numbers and websites

The following are just some of the many organisations and websites which may be useful. Inclusion is not a recommendation.

Institutions and associations

Association for Science Education (ASE) – College Lane, Hatfield, Hertfordshire AL10 9AA. Tel: 01707 283000. www.ase.org.uk

Association of Commonwealth Universities – 36 Gordon Square, London WC1H 0PF. Tel: 020 7380 6700. www.acu.ac.uk

Biochemical Society – Third Floor, Eagle House, 16 Procter Street, London WC1V 6NX. Tel: 0207280 4100. www.biochemsoc.org.uk

British Pharmacological Society – 16 Angel Gate, City Road, London EC1V 2SG. Tel: 020 7417 0113. www.bps.ac.uk

Design and Technology Association (DATA) – Wellesbourne House, Walton Road, Wellesbourne, Warwickshire CV35 9JB. Tel: 01789 470007. www.data.org.uk

e-skills UK Ltd – 1 Castle Lane, London SW1E 6DR. Tel: 020 7963 8920. Represents the IT and telecoms industries. www.e-skills.com

Engineering Council (UK) – 10 Maltravers Street, London WC2R 3ER. Tel: 020 7240 7891. Regulates the engineering profession. www.engc.org.uk

Geological Society – Burlington House, Picadilly, London W1J 0BG. Tel: 020 7434 9944. www.geolsoc.org.uk

Institute of Biology – 9 Red Lion Court, London EC4A 3EF. Tel: 020 7581 8333. www.iob.org

Institute of Biomedical Science – 12 Coldbath Road, London EC1R 5HL. Tel: 020 7713 0214. www.ibms.org

Institute of Mathematics and its Applications – Catherine Richards House, 16 Nelson Street, Southend-on-Sea, Essex SS1 1EF. Tel: 01702 354020. www.ima.org.uk

Institute of Physics – 76 Portland Place, London W1B 1NT. Tel: 020 7470 4800. www.iop.org

Institute of Physics and Engineering in Medicine – Fairmount House, Tadcaster Road, York YO24 1ES. Tel: 01904 610821. www.ipem.ac.uk

International Association for the Exchange of Students for Technical Experience (IAESTE) – Education and Training Group, The British Council, 10 Spring Gardens, London SW1A 2BN. Tel: 020 7389 4774. Organisation that helps university students in science and engineering to find a relevant work experience placement abroad, usually, though not entirely, during the summer vacation. www.iaeste.org

Physiological Society – PO Box 11319, London WC1X 8WQ. Tel: 020 7269 5710. www.physoc.org

Royal Society – 6-9 Carlton House Terrace, London SW1Y 5AG. Tel: 020 7451 2500. The UK national academy for science. www.royalsoc.ac.uk www.sc1.ac.uk

Royal Society of Chemistry – Burlington House, Piccadilly, London W1J 0BA. Tel: 020 7437 8656. www.rsc.org www.chemsoc.org

Campaigns and initiatives

British Association for the Advancement of Science (BA) – Wellcome Wolfson Building, 165 Queen's Gate, London SW7 5HE. Tel: 0870 770 7101. Organises the BA Festival of Science, National Science Week and other events. www.britassoc.org.uk

British Council – Bridgewater House, 58 Whitworth Street, Manchester M1 6BB. Tel: 0161 957 7755. Promotes UK science. www.britishcouncil.org/science

The **Engineering Education Scheme** gives year 12 (Scottish year 5) students the opportunity to work in a team on a real engineering project with a local company.

In England: www.engineering-education.org.uk

In Wales: www.eesw.org.uk

In Scotland: www.scottishengineering.org.uk/courses

In Northern Ireland: www.sentinus.org.uk

Engineering Technology Board – 10 Maltravers Street, London WC2R 3ER. Tel: 020 7240 7333. A partnership which promotes science, engineering and technology. www.etechb.co.uk The ETB has set up a website about careers in these areas: www.scenta.co.uk

The **Headstart** programme – Weltech Centre, Ridgeway, Welwyn Garden City, Hertfordshire AL7 2AA. Tel: 01707 674505. Allows year 12 (Scottish year 5) students to stay at a university for a week to experience the department of engineering at first hand. www.headstartcourses.org.uk

Planet Science – Nesta, Fishmonger Chambers, 110 Upper Thames Street, London EC4R 3TW. Tel: 020 7645 9500. Campaign aimed at stimulating the imagination about science and technology. Focused mainly at young people, parents and teachers in England. www.planet-science.com

Royal Academy of Engineering – 29 Great Peter Street, Westminster, London SW1P 3LW. Tel: 020 7227 0500. A wide range of grants and award schemes for school pupils, undergraduates and those already in engineering/science. Some of the initiatives are listed below. www.raeng.org.uk

Science Engineering Technology Mathematics Network (SETNET) – 2nd Floor, 6 Cavendish Square, London W1G 0PD. Tel: 020 7636 7705. Helpline: 0800 14 64 15. Can provide information on science, engineering and technology careers, national initiatives etc. www.setnet.org.uk

The **Smallpeice Trust** – Holly House, 74 Upper Holly Walk, Leamington Spa, Warwickshire CV32 4JL. Tel: 01926 333200. Offers several schemes and scholarships for 13-18 year olds, including the European Engineering Foundation programme for those over 18 considering an engineering career. It includes academic engineering/ management study, foreign languages and a European work placement. www.smallpeicetrust.org.uk

The **Year in Industry** programme – Technology House, Salford University Business Park, Lisadel Street, Salford M6 6AP. Tel: 0161 278 2497. Offers selected students the chance to gain one year of paid pre-university experience in industry with training. www.yini.org.uk

Qualifications and courses

For information about qualifications up to advanced level:

Qualifications and Curriculum Authority (QCA) – 83 Piccadilly, London W1J 8QA. Tel: 020 7509 5555. www.qca.org.uk

Scottish Qualifications Authority (SQA) – Hanover House, 24 Douglas Street, Glasgow G2 7NQ. Also: Ironmills Road, Dalkeith, Midlothian EH22 1LE. Helpdesk: 0845 279 1000. www.sqa.org.uk

Qualifications, Curriculum and Assessment Authority for Wales (ACCAC) – Castle Buildings, Womanby Street, Cardiff CF10 1SX. Tel: 029 2037 5400. www.accac.org.uk

Northern Ireland Council for the Curriculum, Examinations and Assessment (CCEA) – Clarendon Dock, 29 Clarendon Road, Belfast BT1 3BG. Tel: 028 9026 1200. www.ccea.org.uk

For information about higher education courses:

UCAS (Universities and Colleges Admissions Service) – Rosehill, New Barn Lane, Cheltenham GL52 3LZ. Tel: 0870 112 2211. www.ucas.com

NMAS (Nursing and Midwifery Admissions Service) – address as above for UCAS. Tel: 0870 112 2206. www.nmas.ac.uk

For information about **foundation degrees** and the subjects available: www.foundationdegree.org.uk or www.ucas.com

Women

Association for Women in Science and Engineering – Third Floor, Eagle House, 16 Procter Street, London WC1 6NX. Tel: 020 7060 4571. www.awise.org

The Athena Project – The Royal Society, 6-9 Carlton House Terrace, London SW1Y 5AG. Tel: 020 74512656. Aims to promote the advancement and promotion of careers for women within science engineering and technology in higher education research. www.athenaproject.org.uk

Daphne Jackson Trust – Department of Physics, University of Surrey, Guildford GU2 7XH. Tel: 01483 689166. Provides fellowships that help women returning to a science career following a career break. www.daphnejackson.org.uk

UK Resource Centre for Women in Science, Engineering and Technology – Bradford College, Great Horton Road, Bradford BD7 1AY. Tel: 01274 436485. www.setwomenresource.org.uk

WiTEC – European Association for Women in Science, Engineering and Technology – UK office at Inova Consultancy Ltd, 45a Crescent Road, Sheffield S7 1HL. Tel: 0114 220 7127. www.inovaconsult.com. The European WiTEC organisation's website is www.witec-eu.net

Women Into Science and Engineering (WISE) – 22 Old Queen Street, London SW1H 9HP. Tel: 020 7227 8421. WISE promotes science and engineering careers for girls and women. www.wisecampaign.org.uk

WISE in Northern Ireland. www.wiseni.org

WISE in Wales: Tel: 029 2087 5133. www.wiseinwales.org.uk

WISE in Scotland: Tel: 0131 650 5760. www.girlsgetwise.org.uk

Women's Engineering Society – 22 Old Queen Street, London SW1H 9HP. Tel: 020 7233 1974. A supportive membership organisation for female engineers and students. www.wes.org.uk

Postgraduate study

For information on postgraduate research ratings view the website of **Higher Education & Research Opportunities** in the United Kingdom (HERO): www.hero.ac.uk/rae

Graduate Teacher Training Registry (GTTR) – Rosehill, New Barn Lane, Cheltenham GL52 3LZ. For enquires tel: 01242 544788. Tel: 01242 223707 for an applications pack for postgraduate courses. www.gttr.ac.uk

Possible sources of postgraduate funding

Biotechnology and Biological Sciences Research Council (BBSRC) – Tel: 01793 413200. Covers non-medical life sciences. www.bbsrc.ac.uk

Engineering and Physical Sciences Research Council (EPSRC) – Tel: 01793 444000. Covers physical sciences and engineering. www.epsrc.ac.uk

Natural Environment Research Council (NERC) – Tel: 01793 411500. Covers life, environmental and geological sciences. www.nerc.ac.uk

Particle Physics and Astronomy Research Council (PPARC) – Tel: 01793 442000. Covers particle physics, astronomy, solar system science and particle astrophysics. www.pparc.ac.uk

All the above Research Councils are based at Polaris House, North Star Avenue, Swindon.

Medical Research Council – 20 Park Crescent, London W1B 1AL. Tel: 020 7636 5422. Covers biomedical sciences. www.mrc.ac.uk

Research Councils UK (RCUK) – Tel:01793 444420. Provides information on, and links to, all the Research Councils. www.rcuk.ac.uk

Community Research and Development Information Service (CORDIS) – for information on European research and funding, including schemes to encourage female scientists. www.cordis.lu

Community of Science (COS) – for details of funding opportunities around the world. www.cos.com

Knowledge Transfer Partnerships – Momento House, Harwell, Didcot, Oxfordshire OX11 0QJ. Tel: 0870 190 2829. Devoted to the application of knowledge to business problems and provides funding for research assistantships. www.ktponline.org.uk

Wellcome Trust – Gibbs Building, 215 Euston Road, London NW1 2BE. Tel: 020 7611 8888. www.wellcome.ac.uk

Cancer Research UK – PO Box 123, Lincoln's Inn Fields. London WC2A 3PX. www.science.cancerresearchuk.org

Career Development Loans – promoted by the Learning Skills Council, helpline: 0800 585 505 (for a free information pack and application form). www.lifelonglearning.co.uk also www.support4learning.org.uk

Careers information

NHS Careers Helpline: 0845 60 60 655. www.nhscareers.nhs.uk

Prospects, the UK's official graduate careers website: www.prospects.ac.uk

Careers in information technology also The British Computer Society, 1 Sanford Street, Swindon, Wiltshire SN1 1HJ. Tel: 0845 300 4417. www.bcs.org

Training and Development Agency for Schools – Portland House, Stag Place, London SW1E 5TT. Teaching Information Line: 0845 6000 991. To order a careers booklet phone 0845 606 0323, or view careers and training information on: www.tda.gov.uk

New Scientist – not just a magazine, also a useful website about careers in science: www.newscientist.com

Nature – another magazine with a website about careers in science: www.nature.com

Other useful websites

For careers in engineering: www.enginuity.org.uk

For careers in information technology: www.e-skills.com

For careers for women in information science:www.equalitec.com

Organisation which helps to match students to suitable vacation **work experience**: www.talentladder.com

For information on **school science topics** and their applications: ww.schoolscience.co.uk

MadSci Network – provides answers to science questions and has links to resources on the web: www.madsci.org

Science Magazine has articles on topical science issues and a link to Next Wave, a career development resource for scientists: www.sciencemag.org

Young Engineers – aims to inspire young people to realise the importance and excitement of a career in engineering: www.youngeng.org

Technology Insight allows students to make a 'virtual visit' to industry: www.technology.org.uk

Science Museum in London: www.sciencemuseum.org.uk

New Outlooks in Science and Engineering (Noise) – brings science to life, whether you are thinking about science as a career or want to know more about aspects of science that affect your life: www.noisenet.ws

Novartis Foundation – a charity which aims to promote scientific excellence: www.novartisfound.org.uk

Save British Science Society – a pressure group devoted to improving the health of British science: www.savebritishscience.org.uk

United Nations Educational, Scientific and Cultural Organisations(UNESCO): www.unesco.co.uk

Glossary of science courses

This glossary gives a brief description of the main science subjects offered at universities and colleges of higher education. There are many other higher education courses with variations on these titles. Sometimes this is because the course deals with a specialised branch or application of the subject and sometimes because the course approaches the subject in a particular way. For example, many courses have 'applied' in their title. These usually cover much the same basic theory as the 'pure' courses, but place more emphasis on the applications of the subject and may also include periods of industrial or laboratory experience outside the university.

The title of a course is only a rough guide to what it actually contains, as there can be wide variation in the content of courses with the same title and considerable overlap between courses with different titles. Fuller information about individual courses is available in the *CRAC Degree Course Guides* and *Which Degree?*, and from university and college prospectuses.

All higher education courses in science include some mathematics, statistics and computer methods. Most courses also have practical laboratory work, and fieldwork where appropriate; nearly all courses allow for extended project work in the later stages. Practical work is used to reinforce theoretical work as well as to teach practical techniques and experimental design.

Acoustics – the science of the production and transmission of sound, and its behaviour when it is reflected or absorbed by surfaces. Acoustic engineers are involved with both the enhancement of some sounds, such as from the performers in a theatre or concert hall, and the suppression of others, such as unwanted or environmentally damaging noise. There are important applications in architecture and building, and in areas of mechanical engineering such as aeronautical and automotive engineering, as well as in the music and entertainment industries.

Agricultural science/agriculture – courses normally cover a mixture of the scientific, technological, environmental, practical and business aspects of agriculture, though there is considerable variation in the emphasis given to each component. Several courses require students to have some practical experience of agriculture before the course begins and all have a strong practical element through laboratory and fieldwork projects. The science content is based on chemistry, biochemistry and plant and animal biology. As the courses progress, topics with a more specific application to agriculture are introduced, such as genetics and plant and animal breeding, animal nutrition and physiology, parasitology, stock husbandry and crop and soil science.

Specialised degree courses are available allowing you to study a particular branch of agriculture, such as crop or animal science or production, forestry or horticulture, or the business aspects. Other courses concentrate on a specific area of agricultural science, such as agricultural microbiology, usually with less emphasis on the practical farming content.

Agroforestry – the combined study of agriculture and forestry. As well as studying components of agriculture and forestry separately, there is emphasis on how mixed farming and forestry systems can be sustained in what are often environmentally sensitive areas.

Anatomy/anatomical sciences – the study of the structure of living organisms (although the term 'plant anatomy' is widely used, degree courses in anatomy and anatomical sciences are concerned almost exclusively with mammalian anatomy and in some cases only with human anatomy). Courses emphasise the relationship between structure and function and the way molecular and cellular structures determine macroscopic properties and structures, such as the organisation and function of the body's organs, skeleton, nervous and other systems. Specialised topics within anatomy include histology, embryology (the study of development from the fertilised egg), pathology and the comparative anatomy of different species.

Anatomy degrees do not lead to qualification as a medical doctor. The subject has links with biochemistry, physiology, genetics and microbiology. Anatomy is also an important component of courses in medicine, dentistry, veterinary sciences, human biology and most of the professions allied to medicine, such as physiotherapy and radiography.

Animal science – see zoology

Arboriculture – the breeding and cultivation of trees and shrubs, including planting, pruning, felling, prevention and treatment of diseases and protection from pests. Degree courses in forestry include arboriculture as a major component; they also include wider aspects of forest management and exploitation.

Artificial intelligence – the branch of computer science directed to the solution of problems normally associated with human intelligence. The range of the subject is very large and a wide variety of techniques have been developed for specific application areas, including trying to make computers:

- understand and produce natural human language

- recognise and interpret visual scenes

- capture the knowledge and experience of human experts and then apply them to solving problems – expert or knowledge-based systems

- learn from experience – one technique uses neural networks, which mimic very crudely the way the brain is thought to work.

Techniques in artificial intelligence led to the development of windowing interfaces found on personal computers. Artificial intelligence is a component of many computer science courses but can also be studied in specialist degrees. Artificial intelligence has links with psychology and linguistics.

Astronomy/space science – the scientific study of the universe and the matter it contains, such as the planets, stars and galaxies, the interstellar and intergalactic medium, comets, pulsars, quasars and black holes. Branches of the subject include astrophysics and cosmology (the study of the universe as a whole from its birth in the big bang, through its evolution to its current state, to a variety of conjectured futures). The basis of the subject lies in physics and mathematics. A wide range of observational techniques is used, covering the electromagnetic spectrum from radio waves to gamma rays, with electronic instrumentation and computer interpretation of data playing a major role. Astronomy is taught as a topic in physics degree courses and in specialist degrees. The astrophysics component of astronomy degree courses is often stressed by using the title 'astronomy and astrophysics'.

Astrophysics – the branch of astronomy concerned with using principles from physics to explain astronomical processes. Examples of work done in astrophysics include explaining the production of energy in stars, the evolution of stars over their lifetime, the behaviour of pulsars, the properties of quasars and the nature of the interstellar medium.

Biochemistry – the study of the chemistry of living organisms. The subject covers a very wide range of activities, including:

- investigations into how an organism's metabolism is controlled and supplies energy to the organism

- the operation of processes within the nervous system and brain

- the action of muscles

- the role of hormones and how they control body function

- the operation of the immune system.

A wide range of techniques is used to investigate biochemical reactions, both within the organism and in standard conditions in the laboratory. Techniques are also used to separate, purify, synthesise and modify biomolecules. An important use of the last of these is in genetic engineering, where DNA is manipulated to alter the genetic properties of the organism.

Biochemistry has major applications in medicine, agriculture and, particularly since the development of biotechnology, a wide range of other industries, including pharmaceuticals and the food industry. Biochemistry is also an important component in biology, chemistry, medicine, veterinary science, dietetics, food science, pharmacy and agricultural science degree courses.

Bioinformatics – the application of computer science to biology. Computers have been used increasingly in many areas of biology over recent years. For example, the human genome project has depended heavily on the development and use of computer techniques as well as biological ones. The relative ease with which gene sequencing can now be carried out has led to a very rapid growth in the number and size of biological databases. Advanced computer techniques are now proving essential in the application of genomics to the understanding of how cells and organisms develop and function, and in practical applications such as in the development of new therapies, including the design of more precisely targeted drugs.

Courses in bioinformatics combine topics in both computer science and biology, particularly cell and molecular biology and genetics. Bioinformatics has links with biology, biochemistry, genetics and computer science, and can often be combined with these subjects or taken as an option within them.

Biology (biological science) – the study of living organisms. Biology and biological science degree courses cover a wide range of topics, including plant and animal biology (botany and zoology), biochemistry, cell and molecular biology, genetics and ecology. The vast range of the biological sciences, combined with the phenomenal progress that has been made in some areas, mean that it is impossible to cover all of the subject in depth. Therefore, the later stages of most courses allow specialisation in one or more of the branches just mentioned, or in other specialised topics such as pharmacology, physiology, immunology, toxicology or microbiology. Work in areas such as biotechnology has opened up new areas for the industrial application of biology. Greater awareness of environmental concerns has focused interest on the results produced by the study of ecology. Biology has links with agriculture, medicine, veterinary science, food science and environmental science.

Biomedical science – these courses cover the scientific basis of medicine and draw on many of the biological sciences. The subject is interdisciplinary, combining work in the biological and medical sciences. Courses usually begin by providing a basis in biochemistry, cell and molecular biology and physiology. They build on this with more specialised study in areas such as pharmacology, genetics, nutrition, microbiology, immunology, pathology, neuroscience and even biotechnology in some cases. Some courses are more specifically related to work in hospital medical laboratories, such as medical biochemistry (for the analysis of body fluids), haematology (the study of blood), histology (the study of cells, particularly for cancer diagnosis) and immunology (for detecting antibodies and tissue typing). These courses are a good preparation for work in hospital laboratories and the research laboratories of health and biologically related industries. Some courses are also accredited by the Institute of Biomedical Science and, when they are, the training they give counts towards the requirements for a professional qualification for working in the hospital laboratory service.

Biomedical science has links with biology, biochemistry and medicine.

Biophysics – the study of living organisms, using ideas and methods drawn originally from physics. Work in biophysics includes investigations at the macroscopic scale, such as the mechanics of skeletal and muscle action, but courses now concentrate much more on the cellular and molecular levels, with the use of sophisticated instrumentation techniques. For instance, electronic instrumentation and computer data logging may be used to investigate the cell membrane. At the molecular level, X-ray crystallography and ultraviolet, infra-red and nuclear magnetic resonance spectroscopy are used to investigate and determine three-dimensional molecular structures. Some of these techniques have been adapted for medical use through, for example, computer-aided tomography (CAT scanners). Specialised medical biophysics courses are available. The courses are generally taught in association with other biology courses; the physics content is usually rather less than the biology content and is directed specifically towards biological applications.

Biotechnology – the application of biochemistry, molecular genetics and microbiology to develop industrial applications based on biological processes. Biotechnology is an interdisciplinary subject drawing on results from the biological sciences (particularly biochemistry, microbiology and genetics), chemistry and chemical engineering, so courses cover aspects of all these, though the biological sciences tend to be the largest component. Biotechnology is a rapidly expanding area with great potential for many new and exciting applications in, for example, pharmaceuticals and medicine through the development of new drugs and medical treatments. It is now used in the chemicals industry, in agriculture through the use of genetic engineering to produce improved crops and livestock, and in the food industry, where brewing, for instance, represents an application of biotechnology that existed long before it became established as a separate discipline.

Botany (plant/crop science) – the study of plants or, in some cases, crops. Although botanists have traditionally been concerned primarily with the discovery and classification of new plants, the emphasis is now much more on general principles of cell and molecular biology, plant physiology, ecology and conservation, though the emphasis given to each of these varies from course to course.

Crop science courses are also concerned with practical issues affecting cultivation and protection from disease and pests. Despite the fact that the subject is one of the oldest sciences, new techniques such as cell culture and gene cloning mean that it continues to offer fresh and exciting challenges.

Botany has links with all the other biological sciences, and with agriculture and horticulture.

Cartography – see mapping science

Cell biology – the study of biology at the level of the cell, the fundamental unit of living organisms. Courses include work in biochemistry and molecular biology, which are common to nearly all biological science courses. However, cell biology courses look in much greater detail at cell structure and function, cell membranes, the control, integration and behaviour of cells in multicellular organisms, genetics at the cellular level (cytogenetics) and a variety of techniques such as cell culture.

Ceramics science – the study of ceramics. These are hard, strong materials produced by firing mixtures containing clay. Familiar examples of ceramic materials are pottery, bricks and glazed tiles, but there are many other ceramic materials that are designed to have specific electrical, magnetic and heat-resisting properties that give them a wide variety of industrial and other applications. A well-known example of the use of specialist ceramics is in the space shuttle's re-entry heat shield.

Ceramic science is often taught as part of a materials science or engineering degree course, but is also available as a separate specialist degree course.

Chemical engineering – this is about changing raw materials into useful products, usually by initiating a chemical change. Unlike laboratory chemistry, however, this is achieved in large quantities. Chemical engineers study the design of equipment that is required as part of the chemical process and this relies on a knowledge of thermodynamics, fluid mechanics, heat and mass transfer, separation and filtration techniques, catalysis, fluid motion. The equipment includes reactor vessels where the chemical change takes place, and heat exchangers. The control of chemical plant and attention to potential hazards such as pollution of the environment are an important part of chemical engineers' work. New processes are usually tested using pilot plant where reactions are carried out using small quantities.

Chemical engineers are particularly active in the oil, chemical, biochemical, pharmaceutical, food and water industries. The biochemical industry has been growing rapidly in the last two decades and more emphasis is now placed on biochemical processes.

Chemistry – the study of the properties and reactions of the elements and their compounds. Although the traditional division of chemistry into physical, organic and inorganic tends to be reflected in the organisation of the initial stages of courses, the boundaries between them are not sharp. Specialised options, usually offered later in the courses, do not always fit neatly into this classification. The applications of chemistry are so broad and varied that chemists can be found working in nearly all parts of industry – not only in areas such as chemicals and pharmaceuticals, but also in rather less obvious ones such as the food industry, and wherever materials are produced or processed (for example, in the steel and ceramics industries). Chemists also work in the public sector in analytical laboratories monitoring health and safety. They are at the forefront in the fight against environmental problems – for example, it is chemists who have to find effective alternatives to environmentally harmful substances. Chemistry courses usually provide opportunities to specialise late in the course. However, there are also more specialised degrees, such as biological, medicinal and environmental chemistry, that concentrate on one particular area, though even they usually build from a solid foundation in general chemistry.

Chiropody – see podiatry

Civil engineering – civil engineers are concerned with construction and the built environment. They work on the design and construction of roads, airports, dams, tunnels, high-rise buildings, bridges and much more. Those working for consultants tend to be concerned with initial designs and supervision of contracts while those employed by contractors manage construction projects. Many are employed by the owners of significant engineering works such as local authorities, Network Rail and harbour boards. Key subjects studied by civil engineers include structural mechanics, construction materials, soil mechanics and geotechnics, surveying, hydraulics and environmental engineering. Drawing and sketching also play an important part in the development of design skills.

Computer science/studies – the study of the principles and use of computers. Courses vary greatly, some taking a scientific/mathematical approach, while others concentrate on the practical uses of computers. Many courses have a hardware component covering basic logic circuit design and computer architectures, though more specialised topics such as VLSI (very large-scale integrated circuits) design may also be available as options. The purpose of the hardware component is usually to give a background for other parts of the course. Courses in electronics or electronic engineering may be more suitable for a professional training as a hardware engineer.

The largest amount of time is usually devoted to work on software. All courses cover at least one programming language, and some considerably more. The greatest variation between courses comes from the way they treat applications software. Some concentrate on the low-level software engineering aspects of producing applications, others more on their use in particular areas, such as for business information systems.

Artificial intelligence is a major area of computer science, which some courses cover in considerable depth. They may cover both the basic theory, some of which is drawn from psychology and linguistics, and the use of specific techniques, such as expert systems (also called knowledge-based systems) or neural networks.

Courses vary considerably in how much theory they include and the depth to which they go. The theory has been developed in an attempt to help programmers produce 'correct' programs (in the sense that they behave as intended in all circumstances). The need for this arises from the fact that only very small programs can be tested exhaustively. The theory uses ideas and notation drawn from mathematics; in its more advanced forms it is highly mathematical.

Courses in the area of computer science are available under a number of other titles, such as 'computing', 'information technology' and 'business computer systems', which usually reflect a more specialised orientation. Many other subjects include topics in the use of computers, though they are usually only concerned with the use of methods and applications relevant to that subject.

Crop science – see botany

Cybernetics – the study of systems and how they are controlled. Applications include industrial automation and robotics. Techniques are drawn from a wide area, including electronics, computer science, artificial intelligence and instrumentation.

Dentistry – dentists work to conserve their patients' teeth and to treat problems of decay, gum disease and misalignment if they arise. The courses last five years and involve considerable clinical practice. The basic content of all courses is very similar, but courses differ in the way they are organised, the emphasis given to different elements and the possibilities for elective studies in the later stages of the course.

Dietetics – the scientific study of diet and nutrition. Courses with 'dietetics' in their title usually provide a period of professional training in hospitals, and can lead to state registration, which is required for professional practice as a dietitian in the National Health Service. Dietitians also work in the food industry and in private practice. Courses include components of physiology, biochemistry and microbiology, together with elements drawn from the behavioural and social sciences.

Earth science – an interdisciplinary subject combining the study of geology (the largest component) with aspects of physical geography and, in some cases, oceanography, meteorology and climatology.

Ecology – the study of the interrelationships between plants and animals, and between them and their environment. It looks at how the environment influences, and is influenced by, individual organisms, populations of an individual species and communities of different species. Ecology is normally taught alongside other biological science courses and often shares with them a basic grounding in topics such as plant and animal biology, cell and molecular biology and genetics. Issues of conservation and environmental damage through pollution and other factors are usually covered. The later stages of courses often allow some specialisation in the study of specific ecosystems, such as marine, freshwater, or agricultural ecology.

As well as being available as a specialist degree subject, ecology is taught in many biological science courses. It is also a major component in environmental science courses with a biological science orientation; specialised ecology courses generally give less emphasis to social and policy issues.

Electrical engineering – this is concerned with all the applications of electricity that use high current. This includes the generation of electricity using turbine generators and its distribution around the national grid. Electrical engineers are actively involved in the search for, and development of, alternative sources of energy such as wind and wave power and solar energy, and the development of electric cars as opposed to oil-powered vehicles. Electrical engineers are involved in design, installation, testing and maintenance of electric railways and the supply of current to industrial plant and for heating and lighting. Most degree courses include both electrical and electronic engineering, and electrical engineers have knowledge of electronic control systems for the control of electrical devices.

Electronic engineering – our modern living is entirely reliant on electronics. Computers, telecommunications, medical imaging, hi-fi, control systems, seismic exploration for oil, navigation and numerous other applications all rely on electronics. Electronic circuits are designed and placed on 'chips' as integrated circuits. Increasingly large circuits can now be placed on ever smaller 'chips' to run ever smaller computers, mobile phones and other pieces of equipment. Digital systems are taking over from analogue, optical systems using lasers and optical fibre sometimes replacing electrons and copper wire. Wireless systems are being developed so that, for example, a computer, printer, scanner and other equipment can communicate with each other by radio without the need of wires.

Electronics – the study of the construction and use of electronic devices. These devices are now almost exclusively semiconductor-based. Courses usually give a balanced treatment of both linear (analogue) and digital electronics, though some more specialised courses are available. A wide range of applications is normally covered from areas such as instrumentation, telecommunications, control systems, computer design and architecture, and audio-electronics. Electronics is available as a specialist topic within other subjects, such as physics and mechanical engineering. Some courses, which also cover the generation and distribution of electricity, are called electrical and electronic engineering.

Environmental health – the courses are concerned with the health implications of environmental factors such as food safety, pollution and noise. Courses cover the relevant basic science, such as microbiology, anatomy and environmental studies, as well as more specific topics, such as food safety and hygiene, and occupational health and safety. They also cover the relevant legislation and how it is enforced. Qualified environmental health officers work mainly for local authorities to improve standards of health and safety, particularly in food production and service, but also in other aspects of people's living and working environments.

Environmental science/studies – an interdisciplinary subject studying the environment and the very wide range of factors affecting it. The content and emphasis of courses varies considerably. Some courses have a physical sciences (most particularly, chemistry) or earth science orientation; rather more have a biological sciences bias and others a balance of approaches, though in the latter case options may allow some specialisation in a particular area. Many of the courses with a biological orientation may share appreciable content with courses in ecology, but tend to be more concerned with practical and social issues, and the resulting consequences for policy. This means that many courses also include relevant aspects of law, economics and other social sciences. There is a wide variety of courses specialising in specific aspects of the subject, such as environmental management, environmental chemistry, environmental biology or environmental toxicology (pollution).

Ergonomics – the study of human beings in their working environment and, in particular, the design of working practices, equipment and tools for optimum efficiency and protection of workers' health and safety. Courses include relevant aspects of anatomy, psychology, physiology, industrial engineering and design. Issues dealt with include furniture design, factory and office layout, and environmental conditions such as heating and lighting.

Food science/studies – the scientific study of food, including its production, processing, storage and distribution as well as nutrition. Food science courses are firmly based on chemistry and biochemistry, with contributions from microbiology and physiology. Food studies courses usually have a less intensive science content and give more emphasis to the general aspects of food, such as related economic and social issues. Both types of course include topics relevant to management in the food industry, though there are also specialised courses dealing with business aspects of the food industry, such as food marketing, which often include some work on food science.

Forestry – courses cover all aspects of the cultivation, exploitation and management of forests. Building on a foundation of basic science, including chemistry, geology, botany, zoology and soil science, they cover more specialised topics such as wood structure, tree and forest husbandry (silviculture), tree pests and diseases, forest measurement, land use and urban forestry, together with economics and management. There is a strong emphasis on practical work and prominence is given to commercial as well as technical aspects.

Genetics – the study of the inheritable characteristics of organisms. Initially, genetics was concerned with the study of the development of genetic variation in whole populations. Although this still plays a part, the emphasis of courses is now much more at the cellular and molecular level, where an understanding of the structure of DNA and the way it can be manipulated allows the possibility of changing the genetic make-up of organisms through the techniques of genetic engineering. The scientific, medical and commercial applications of these techniques are immense and only just beginning to be realised. Courses in human genetics often cover the topic of genetic counselling, which requires technical, social and personal skills.

Genetics courses are often taught in parallel with other biological science courses, with much of the content shared in the early stages. Genetics is also taught as part of courses in other biological sciences, medicine, veterinary science, agriculture and horticulture.

Geochemistry – the chemistry of rocks and the processes occurring during rock formation and transformation. Chemistry is an important tool for the geologist, providing both a method of identification through analysis and the means for explaining many of the properties of rocks and the processes taking place during their formation. Geochemistry is therefore often an important component of geology courses, but specialist courses are also available allowing for deeper treatment of the subject. Geochemical prospecting is used commercially to find deposits of ores from analyses of soils, water courses and sediments.

Geological science – courses combine work in geology, geophysics, geochemistry and applied geology.

Geology – the study of the Earth, including its composition, structure and historical development from its creation five billion years ago to the present day. Geologists study the rocks appearing at the surface of the Earth, but also use less direct evidence, such as the way seismic waves are transmitted within the Earth. The theory of plate tectonics has had a major influence on geology in recent decades and is used as a unifying concept in many courses. Geology courses draw on a wide range of basic sciences, and cover many different topics, including:

- crystallography

- mineralogy – the study of the crystalline material that forms rocks

- petrology – the study of rock origin, composition, structure and alteration

- geochemistry

- geophysics

- stratigraphy – the study of strata laid down over time

- palaeontology – the study of fossils.

The applications of geology to oil and mineral prospecting and extraction are obvious, but it is also important for civil engineering projects, such as tunnel boring and the building of dams and reservoirs. A knowledge of the geology of the area is also important for the analysis of environmental problems, such as the flow of pollutants from ground water to water courses or drinking water. Geology is a major component of earth science courses and some courses in environmental science.

Geophysics – the study of the physical properties of the Earth (and by extension, other planets). By studying these properties, geophysicists are able to deduce the structure of the Earth and the nature of processes within it at great depths beneath the surface. Geophysicists draw on and develop a wide range of physics, including theories of fluid and heat flow, electromagnetism, gravitation and wave propagation through solids and fluids. Data is gathered using sophisticated electronic instrumentation, including instruments based on satellites and space probes. Computers are used extensively to control instruments, process the data and then interpret it through the use of complex mathematical models. Geophysicists make a major contribution to the search for oil and minerals. They are also involved in work on earthquakes, which may, in time, enable them to give reliable predictions of when and where they will occur. Geophysics topics appear in most geology and some physics courses.

Health studies – covers a variety of different courses where biological and medical subjects are combined with social studies, health administration and, in some courses, sports management and administration. The courses are often part of combined or modular degrees with a wide choice of options.

Horticulture – the cultivation of plants for food (commercial horticulture) or to enhance the environment (amenity horticulture). Courses start with a foundation in basic science, usually including botany/plant science, biochemistry, soil science, ecology and genetics. They then introduce more specialist horticultural topics, such as plant production, plant pests and diseases, crop protection, landscape management and the use of organic methods. All courses place strong emphasis on practical work and prominence is given to commercial as well as technical aspects throughout. There is usually a wide range of options in the final year and it is often possible to specialise in commercial or amenity horticulture at that stage.

Horticulture has links with the biological sciences, forestry and agriculture.

Immunology – the study of the system used by organisms as a protection against infection. The function of the immune system has been recognised for many years and this enabled the discovery of vaccines. More recently, however, there has been growing interest in the immune system and problems connected with it. One reason for this was the development of transplant surgery, where the immune system must be counteracted to prevent the rejection of the transplanted tissue. A class of diseases called auto-immune diseases, which includes rheumatoid arthritis, has also been recognised. In these, the immune system malfunctions and acts against the body's own tissues. There are also conditions and diseases, such as AIDS, where the immune system breaks down and leaves the body unprotected against infection.

The courses are closely linked with the biological sciences and medicine, and develop from a foundation including biochemistry, physiology and cell and molecular biology. Immunology can be studied in a specialist degree course or as part of a course in biological science, medicine or veterinary science.

Information management/science – the study of the collection, storage, retrieval and dissemination of information. Information management courses are now largely concerned with the creation and use of computer-based information systems. Some, however, do still include more traditional areas of library work and may lead to professional qualifications in librarianship. This means that the courses are now less distinct from other courses directed at the information industry, such as information systems and information technology.

Information technology – this title is used for two rather different types of computing course. The first type has an engineering orientation with rather more emphasis on hardware, particularly in connection with communications and networks, than is usual in computer science courses. The second type of course is concerned mainly with the use of business or management software systems, with less emphasis on low-level programming and hardware than in most computer science courses. Courses with titles such as business information technology are usually of this second type, but in general the only way of telling the orientation of a specific course is from a detailed description of its contents.

Linguistics – the scientific study of language and its structure. This includes the way sounds are used to make speech (phonetics and phonology), the way sentences are constructed (syntax), the way meaning is conveyed using words and sentences (semantics) and the way language is used in context (pragmatics). Linguistics is also a component of some courses in foreign languages, speech science, education, computer science (particularly artificial intelligence) and psychology.

Mapping science (cartography) – the study of the processes required for the creation of maps. The process of creating a map can be divided into data acquisition, analysis and presentation. One aspect of data acquisition is surveying, which includes land-based and remote sensing using aerial and satellite imaging. However, since maps are used to display a wide range of information, including such things as market research results, data acquisition also covers issues such as social survey and sampling techniques. The analysis phase includes image analysis and processing, as well as statistical analysis. The presentation stage covers a wide range from manual mapping to the construction of computer-based geographical information systems.

Mapping science is often a component of degrees in surveying, geography and geology.

Marine biology – the study of the biological systems found in the sea, including individual organisms and a variety of ecosystems. The courses build from a solid foundation in biological science, covering basic plant and animal biology, cell biology, biochemistry, ecology, genetics and evolution. An understanding of the marine environment is gained through the study of physical, chemical and atmospheric processes within and around the sea and oceans. More specialised courses build on this work. Topics cover the physiology of marine organisms, food chain processes, behaviour, marine pollution, conservation, fisheries and aquaculture.

Marine biology is also available in combination with freshwater biology and as a specialised option in some biology/biological science courses.

Materials science – the study of the physical properties of natural and man-made materials used in industry and construction. Many of the advances that have led to an increase in the standard of living this century have been brought about by a greater understanding of the way materials can be used, and by the introduction of new materials with improved properties or lower production costs. For example, much of the engineering industry relies on the use of high-performance alloys.

Courses cover a wide range of materials, which may include natural materials such as wood or stone, though the emphasis is more commonly on artificial or processed materials such as ceramics, metals, semiconductors and plastics. Particularly active areas of the subject include the production of new semiconductors offering greatly enhanced computer performance and the development of high-temperature superconductors. The courses draw from a variety of other subjects but are principally based on solid state physics and chemistry. Some courses allow the specialised study of individual materials from the start of the course, while others begin with a more general approach, though usually allow specialisation later.

Materials science is also a major part of materials engineering degree courses and is often a component of mechanical engineering courses.

Mathematics – a broad and diverse subject with a history dating back to 3000 BC, but one that is developing more rapidly now than at any time in the past. There are some broad divisions within the subject, which you can concentrate on by taking a specialist degree or by taking options in a general mathematics degree. Pure mathematics includes topics that have familiar titles, such as calculus, algebra and geometry though the content of the last two in particular is markedly different from what you have experienced at school. It also includes topics that are less familiar, such as logic, ring and field theory, number theory and topology. Applied mathematics includes topics such as mechanics, electromagnetic field theory, fluid mechanics, relativity and quantum theory and elementary particle physics. Applicable mathematics includes a variety of techniques that are used widely in business and covers topics in statistics and methods of optimisation such as linear programming. Statistics is also a component of many mathematics courses.

Virtually all courses include some computer science. There are many specialist mathematics courses dealing with particular application areas, such as business mathematics or mathematical physics. All science and engineering courses include some mathematics.

Mechanical engineering – concerned with the design, development, manufacture and testing of any object that has moveable parts, from an aeroplane to a washing machine, or a heart pacemaker to a computer keyboard. The selection of materials and knowledge of how they behave under stress is an important factor in the design of any article. Fracture mechanics, welding and methods of joining materials together, and tribology – the study of surfaces and how they wear when in dynamic contact with each other – are all a part of this subject. Students learn the fundamental principles of engineering, how to design articles and manufacturing methods. There is a strong mathematical element and computer control of mechanical equipment is usually included in courses.

Medical physics – the study of the interaction between the body and all types of radiation used for diagnostic and therapeutic purposes. Diagnostic techniques include X-rays, ultrasound scans, gamma-ray imaging and magnetic resonance imaging. Therapeutic techniques include laser surgery and radiation treatment. Courses start with a foundation of mathematics and physics, including electromagnetism, atomic physics, nuclear physics and optical physics. This forms the basis for the study of more specialised topics such as biophysics, physiological medicine and radiography.

Medical physics options are available in the later stages of several physics courses. There are also medical electronics courses, which concentrate on physiological monitoring and instrumentation.

Medicine – courses leading to professional qualification as doctors. The courses last five or six years, though there are some special four-year courses for those who have already graduated in another discipline. They are based on a foundation in basic medical science subjects including human anatomy and physiology, biochemistry, microbiology, pharmacology, genetics, immunology and pathology. The remainder of the course is devoted to clinical training, though some formal teaching continues throughout the course. In most courses the non-clinical and clinical aspects are now more integrated, and there is usually some clinical contact from the start of the course.

Able students may be allowed to extend their studies by spending an extra year in the middle of the course studying some aspect of medical science in greater depth. These 'intercalated years' lead to the award of an additional degree. Courses usually contain an elective period towards the end when students can broaden their experience by performing a research project or gaining clinical experience in a new environment, such as in a foreign country. At the end of the course, a further year of experience leads to registration with the General Medical Council, but several years' further training is required before appointment to a permanent post in hospital medicine or general practice.

There are also other degree courses allied to medicine, leading directly to professions such as chiropractic, osteopathy, and prosthetics and orthotics.

Metallurgy – the study of the extraction, purification, production and properties of metals. Metals play a vital part in all areas of industry, especially in areas such as engineering and construction. Metallurgists ensure that metals have the correct properties to perform the task required effectively and safely. They create high-performance alloys for special purposes in industries such as aerospace, as well as ensuring, for instance, that the quality of steel used in car manufacturing is consistent. The way in which metals are affected by exposure to the elements depends on their properties, which in turn depend on their constituents and the way they are processed. Metallurgy courses draw on material from a wide range of other subjects including chemistry, physics, geology and crystallography in order to understand these relationships.

Metallurgy is also available as part of materials science/engineering courses, and has links with mechanical and other engineering degrees.

Meteorology – the scientific study of the weather and atmospheric processes. The behaviour of the atmosphere is extremely complex and meteorologists have to draw on a wide range of information, techniques and theories. Courses include physics and mathematics, and topics such as atmospheric dynamics, atmospheric physics, climate change, surface processes and oceanography. The meteorologist uses acquired knowledge to build sophisticated mathematical models and computer simulations to understand and predict evolving weather patterns.

Meteorology is available as a single honours course, but is more frequently combined with mathematics or physics, or taken as part of a course in environmental or earth science. A degree in physics or maths can also lead to a career in meteorology.

Microbiology – the scientific study of micro-organisms, including bacteria, viruses, protozoa and some algae and fungi considered small enough to qualify. The courses are often taught alongside other biological science courses and often share with them a basic grounding in topics such as plant and animal biology, biochemistry, cell and molecular biology, genetics and ecology. This leads to more specialised topics such as bacteriology, virology, mycology (the study of fungi) and immunology. Courses often have a range of options related to the application of microbiology to agriculture and medicine. The importance of microbes as agents of disease has long been recognised, but the explosion of interest in biotechnology in recent years has given extra impetus to the study of microbiology. For example, bacteria can be genetically engineered so that they produce human enzymes or hormones. The bacteria can then be grown on an industrial scale to produce these compounds commercially for medical use.

Microbiology is also available as a component of degrees in biological sciences, medicine, veterinary science, dentistry, horticulture and agriculture.

Midwifery – midwives are trained to meet the needs of childbearing women and their families who come from varying cultural and socio-economic backgrounds. They work in hospitals and clinics as well as visiting patients at home. Their role goes much further than delivering babies. They are involved in antenatal and postnatal care, in counselling, offering support and education and in helping mothers and their partners prepare for parenthood. The role includes working in partnership with other health professionals, making clinical examinations and providing health and patent education. Some enter the career of midwife directly and others after qualifying as a nurse. The National Health Service pays for all student course fees.

Molecular biology – the study of the structure and reactions of large biological molecules such as nucleic acids and proteins. The courses are often taught alongside other biological science courses and often share with them a basic grounding in topics such as chemistry, biochemistry, plant and animal biology, cell biology and genetics. Other topics that may be taught later in the course include microbiology, immunology and biotechnology. Molecular biology is at the centre of many of the most exciting developments in biology and its influence has spread to many other branches of the subject, such as genetics. The scientific, medical and commercial applications of genetic engineering have created even greater interest in the subject.

Molecular biology is often combined with cell biology and is also available as a component of degrees in biological science, biochemistry and agriculture.

Neuroscience – the study of the nervous system, including the brain. Neuroscience draws on a wide range of other biological and medical subjects, including molecular biology, cell biology (to study the chemical and electrical communications between cells), and psychology (to study the behaviour of the whole organism). Because of this, the courses normally begin with a solid foundation of biochemistry, animal biology, cell and molecular biology, pharmacology and physiology. Understanding the function of the brain is one of the most challenging problems in modern biology and medicine, with many potential applications. Neuroscience is available as a single honours course, but is more frequently taken as an option towards the end of physiology courses.

Nursing/nursing studies – degree courses that include professional nursing training. Most courses last three years, but some last four years. The courses begin with a common foundation programme (CFP) lasting 12-18 months, followed by a branch programme in one of the four nursing branches: adult, mental health, learning disability or children's nursing. The CFP is designed to develop the nursing skills of observation, communication and caring as well as to teach medical science topics based on anatomy, physiology, pharmacology and human development. The CFP also includes an introduction to the four nursing branches and to maternity care. After the CFP, the specialised branch programme is spent largely in hospital and community-based supervised nursing practice.

In addition to these three or four year pre-registration nursing degrees, there are some one- or two-year degree courses for students who are already qualified nurses.

Nutrition – the study of the body's requirements for food and how they can be met. The courses are often similar to, and taught with, courses in dietetics, except that they do not have a period of professional practice or lead to professional registration as a dietitian. There are also a number of courses in animal nutrition, which are taught alongside agricultural sciences. Nutrition can also be studied as part of courses in physiology, food science and agriculture.

Occupational health and safety – the study of health and safety at work and in the wider environment, and how it can be maintained and improved. Subjects studied include physiology, pathology, ergonomics, occupational health, environmental measurement methods, toxicology, law and risk management. These courses are specialised training for jobs in health and safety advice and inspection.

Occupational therapy – the courses provide professional training for occupational therapists. Qualified occupational therapists are employed in hospitals to help people overcome the effects of mental or physical illnesses or disability so that they can live as full and independent lives as possible. The courses cover human biology, psychology, anatomy and physiology, as well as the principles and techniques of treatment. All the courses include practical work with patients suffering from physical and/or psychological difficulties or disabilities, and draw on personal and social skills as well as technical knowledge.

Oceanography – the scientific study of the oceans. Oceanography is a very broad subject drawing on many other disciplines. For example, understanding the intricate patterns of ocean currents, tides and waves requires complex computer models drawing on theories of fluid flow from physics and mathematics. Studies of the sea floor apply knowledge from geology. Marine chemists study interactions at the interfaces between sea water and materials in the sea bed, and sea water and the atmosphere at the surface. Marine biologists investigate all aspects of life in the sea. The practical importance of understanding the oceans is immense. For instance, the oceans have been used to absorb vast amounts of waste material, and only with a proper understanding of processes within the oceans can the resulting risks be assessed. The oceans are a major food resource and support major transport systems. Oil is already being taken from below the sea bed and there is potential for extracting other materials. The oceans also have a major effect on climate.

Oceanography can also be studied as part of a course in earth science or geophysics.

Optometry (ophthalmic optics) – the courses provide professional training for optometrists (also called ophthalmic opticians). Optometrists carry out eye tests to detect abnormalities and vision defects, analyse the results, and prescribe and dispense spectacles and contact lenses.

Optometrists also carry out work in orthoptics and check for diseases of the eye such as glaucoma, referring patients to specialist doctors (ophthalmic surgeons) for treatment. The courses include the anatomy and physiology of the eye, optics, clinical optometry (measurement), methods of examination and diseases of the eye, as well as clinical work with patients. They also draw on personal and social skills and technical knowledge.

Orthoptics – the diagnosis and treatment of disorders of the eye caused by problems with the muscles controlling the eye. The courses provide professional training in orthoptics. Much of the orthoptist's work is with young children, dealing with squints, for example, but they also work with adults suffering from a variety of conditions such as the after-effects of accidents and strokes. Orthoptists can treat some of the problems they diagnose, but refer more severe cases to specialist doctors (ophthalmic surgeons). The courses include the anatomy and physiology of the eye, optics, child development and ophthalmology (the scientific study of the eye). The courses also include clinical work with patients and draw on personal and social skills as well as technical knowledge.

Pathology – the study of disease and disease-causing micro-organisms such as bacteria and viruses. It includes the study of microscopic and macroscopic changes in the organisation of tissues, and chemical changes in tissues and body fluids. The courses start with the study of healthy organisms and progress to contrasting them with those affected by disease. Anatomy, physiology, cell biology, genetics and microbiology, as well as more specialised topics such as cell pathology and haematology (the study of cells circulating in the bloodstream) are included on courses.

Pathology is available as a single honours course, but is more frequently taken as a component of courses in biological and biomedical science, medicine, veterinary science and agricultural science. To become a professional pathologist, you must first qualify as a doctor.

Pharmacology – the study of the action of drugs on living systems. Courses build from a foundation of chemistry, biochemistry, cell and molecular biology, physiology and pathology. In addition, there are specialist topics within pharmacology, such as the mechanisms of drug action and drug toxicity. Pharmacologists are involved in medical research and play a vital role in the pharmaceuticals industry, helping with the development and screening of new drugs for use in medicine, veterinary science and agriculture.

Pharmacology is also studied as a component in some agriculture, biochemistry and biological science courses, and is an integral part of the training for pharmacy, medicine, veterinary science, dentistry and nursing. Indeed, many professional pharmacologists originally trained in medicine or pharmacy.

Pharmacy – the courses provide professional training for pharmacists. About one-third of the course is spent studying pharmacology. The rest of the time is used to study basic subjects, such as chemistry and microbiology, as well as more specialised topics, such as:

- pharmaceutical chemistry – the structural analysis and synthesis of drugs

- pharmaceutics – the manufacture of drugs and their formulation into a suitable form for humans or animals

- clinical pharmacology – the study of the effects of drugs on the human body.

Other subjects that may be studied include toxicology (the study of poisons) and pharmaceutical engineering. In addition to working in retail pharmacies, pharmacists are also employed in hospital pharmacies and the pharmaceutical industry.

Physics – the science concerned with the behaviour and properties of matter and energy, but largely excluding those processes involving a change in chemical composition. Physics encompasses investigations at the smallest possible scale of sub-elementary particles called quarks, as well as explanations of the origin and evolution of the entire universe, using general relativity. Indeed, attempts are now being made to explain both these extremes within a single unified theory. There remain many challenging fundamental problems left for the physicist in areas such as low-temperature physics, solid-state physics, plasma physics and astrophysics, as well as in other areas where the techniques of physics are applied, such as medical physics and geophysics.

Courses usually build from a solid foundation of classical physics covering topics such as mechanics, electromagnetism, properties of matter, thermodynamics and statistical mechanics. To these are added quantum mechanics and relativity, which were developed in the early years of the twentieth century and revolutionised the way physicists and others viewed the world. They are still the two key theories of modern physics. In the later stages of courses, more specialised topics can usually be studied, such as nuclear physics, astronomy, astrophysics, biophysics, geophysics, X-ray crystallography, medical physics, elementary particle physics, electronics and laser physics.

Mathematics is also an important component of all physics courses, particularly those with options in theoretical physics. Physics topics are also studied within all engineering, electronics and applied mathematics courses.

Physiology – the study of how animals function (plant physiology appears as a title for topics in botany and biological science courses, but you can assume that courses called physiology are only concerned with animal, and often just vertebrate, physiology). Physiology covers all levels, from the subcellular, such as the operation of cell membranes, through the function of individual organs, such as the way the heart operates as a pump, up to the way the animal functions as a whole. In explaining how organisms function, physiology draws on ideas and techniques from a wide range of other subjects, including physics and chemistry, and many of the biological sciences, such as anatomy, biochemistry, genetics, pharmacology and microbiology.

Physiology can also be studied within courses in biological science, human biology and agriculture, and is an important component of courses in medicine, dentistry, veterinary science and most of the professions allied to medicine, such as physiotherapy and radiography.

Physiotherapy – the courses provide professional training for physiotherapists. Qualified physiotherapists work in hospitals and the community. They use physical methods including manipulation, massage, infrared heat treatment and remedial exercises to treat clients of all ages who may be suffering from any of a wide range of disabilities and disorders, such as arthritis, mental illness, stroke and accidents. Courses include anatomy, physiology, pathology, human science, biomechanics and treatment techniques. All the courses include clinical work with clients and draw on personal and social skills as well as technical knowledge.

Plant science – see botany

Podiatry (Chiropody) – the diagnosis, treatment and management of conditions affecting the foot and lower limb. Courses provide professional training that can lead to state registration, which is required for employment in the National Health Service. Clinical practice is an important part of all courses and can occupy up to half of the time. Theoretical work covers the structure and function of the normal limb, the biomechanics of locomotion and gait, pathology, podiatric medicine, behavioural science and treatment techniques. Qualified podiatrists work in hospitals and the community, in both the National Health Service and private practice.

Polymer science – the study of polymers (molecules made up of long chains of repeating units), including their formation, properties and uses. Polymeric materials come in many different forms, such as plastics, fibres and foams; they may be synthetic, such as nylon or polystyrene, or natural, such as rubber or cellulose. It is possible to fine tune the properties of polymers in the manufacturing process, so they can often be adapted for different applications. They can also be combined with other materials to form composites that display the best properties of each material. The courses are specialised materials science courses, and are often taught alongside other materials science courses with which they share some common content.

Polymer science can also be studied as a component of courses in materials science and chemistry, though the approach in the latter will be rather different.

Psychology – the scientific study of the mind. Psychology is a very broad subject and different courses may emphasise very different aspects. One reflection of this is that it may be offered as a BSc within a science or social science faculty or a BA within an arts faculty, though, if they are offered at the same institution, much of the teaching may be common.

Courses also vary in the amount of work on animals, as well as in the emphasis given to different branches of psychology, such as:

- experimental psychology

- cognitive psychology – the study of thought processes, memory and language

- physiological psychology – the study of the relationship between brain function and psychological processes

- comparative psychology – the study of animal behaviour and the similarities and differences between species

- developmental psychology – changes in psychological processes during maturation into adulthood

- social psychology – how people and animals behave in groups

- the psychology of individual differences – the study of factors such as personality and intelligence

- abnormal psychology – the study of abnormal behaviour

■ applied psychology – the application of psychology to practical problems, for example in negotiation strategies.

Psychology can also be studied in a wide variety of other courses, including education, medicine and the professions allied to medicine, such as nursing and occupational therapy.

Graduates who wish to become professional psychologists need to complete a course that is accredited by the British Psychological Society. Postgraduate training is required to enter the key occupations of clinical, educational, occupational and forensic psychology.

Radiography – the courses provide professional training in diagnostic or therapeutic radiography, and can lead to state registration, which is required for employment in the National Health Service. The two branches of the profession are distinct and the courses separate, though some teaching may be common to both. Diagnostic radiographers work in the X ray departments of hospitals or in health centres. They use a wide variety of techniques, including X-rays, ultrasound, magnetic resonance and radionucleotide imaging, and computer-aided tomography to produce images to help doctors perform diagnoses. Therapeutic radiographers work in hospital clinical oncology (cancer) departments. They plan and administer treatment using a variety of radiation sources such as X-rays, isotopes and linear accelerators. Both types of course include anatomy, physiology, pathology, radiographic physics, radiographic techniques, patient care and professional practice as radiographers. All the courses include clinical work with patients and draw on personal and social skills as well as technical knowledge.

Speech sciences/speech therapy – the study of speech, including anatomy and physiology of the mouth and throat, phonetics (vocal sounds), linguistics (the structure of language), psychology and the pathology of speech problems. Other topics covered include acoustics, audiology, neurology and education. Speech therapy courses also include clinical practice and contribute to a professional qualification in the diagnoses and treatment of speech defects. Speech therapists work with children in schools and clinics, and with adults with speech problems, such as stroke patients.

Sports science – the study of human movement, physiology, anatomy and psychology in relation to sporting activities. Many courses also include topics on the management of sports facilities.

Statistics – the science of collecting and analysing numerical data. Statistics is a major branch of mathematics with applications in practically every area of scientific, commercial and administrative activity. For example, the results of any scientific experiment must be shown to be statistically valid before they are accepted; the demand for new products has to be assessed before they are launched; and the provision of education and health services has to be planned in advance to cope with changes in population and technology. Courses cover a range of basic mathematical subjects such as calculus and algebra, as well as more specialised topics such as probability analysis, statistical distributions and a wide range of statistical analysis techniques. The use of computers is essential for the statistician, so courses include numerical analysis and computer science, with particular emphasis on the use of a wide range of software packages for statistical analysis in various fields.

Statistics can also be studied in combination with mathematics or as part of a mathematics degree. Topics in statistics are also taught in all science and medical degree courses and form important components of courses in the social sciences, such as psychology and business studies. Statisticians are employed in all areas of science but also in market research, financial analysis and actuarial work.

Veterinary sciences – the courses provide professional training in veterinary medicine. Courses last five or six years and include many similar subjects to medical degrees, such as anatomy, biochemistry, physiology, medicine, surgery, obstetrics, pharmacology and pathology, though the focus is naturally on animals rather than humans. Courses cover large animal (farm livestock) and small animal (domestic pets) practice, as well as some exotic animals. Practical clinical training is a major component of all courses and dominates the second half of the course. It is usually carried out in clinics attached to the veterinary school and by attachment to practising veterinarians. Experience of practical work with livestock on a farm is also part of the training.

Zoology (animal science) – the scientific study of animals, including their anatomy, physiology, classification, distribution, behaviour and ecology. Courses often run alongside other courses in biological science and share with them a foundation in biochemistry, cell and molecular biology, microbiology and genetics. Many courses stress the practical importance of zoology, with specialist topics such as fisheries biology and parasitology. In fact, some animal science courses are directed specifically towards agricultural applications.

Zoology can also be studied as a component of courses in biological science, agriculture and environmental science.

More titles in the Student Helpbook series ...

helping students of all ages make the right choices about their careers and education.

New edition
Careers with an Arts or Humanities Degree
Published in association with UCAS
Compulsory reading for anyone considering arts or humanities at degree level.
£10.99   ISBN: 1 904979 06 8

A Year Off ... A Year On?
Published in association with UCAS
All the information and advice you need on how to make the most of your time out between courses or jobs.
£10.99   ISBN: 1 902876 86 5

New edition
Student Life: A Survival Guide
Published in association with UCAS
Essential advice for students beginning or soon to begin university or college; includes invaluable help on how to budget and get the most out of their time.
£10.99   ISBN: 1 904979 01 7

Jobs and Careers after A levels and equivalent advanced qualifications
Opportunities for students leaving school or college at 18, including advice on job-hunting, applications and interviews.
£10.99   ISBN: 1 902876 93 8

CVs and Applications
For anyone who is applying for a job or college place; includes details of how to use the internet in marketing yourself.
£10.99   ISBN: 1 902876 81 4

Excel at Interviews
This highly successful book makes invaluable reading for students and jobhunters.
£10.99   ISBN: 1 902876 82 2

Visit us online to view our full range of resources at:
www.lifetime-publishing.co.uk